1908 ~ 1998

90th Anniversary of the Old Age
Pension Act

How The Pension Was Won ~
The Forgotten Story

NO THANKS TO LLOYD GEORGE

Dave Goodman

Foreword by Jack Jones

Third Age Press

ISBN 1 898576 12 2
Second edition

Third Age Press Ltd, 1998
Third Age Press, 6 Parkside Gardens
London SW19 5EY
Managing Editor Dianne Norton

© Dave Goodman

Punch cartoons reproduced with the permission of Punch Ltd
Photographs from *How Old Age Pensions Began To Be* by
Francis Herbert Stead, 1910 Methuen
Cover photograph by courtesy of The Mansell Collection
Stead plaque photo by Stan Gamester

Layout design by Dianne Norton
Printed and bound in Great Britain
by Watkiss Studios

How The Pension Was Won ~ The Forgotten Story

NO THANKS TO LLOYD GEORGE

*This edition is dedicated
to the memory of my wife,
Moyra,
whose contribution to it
was invaluable
and
to the late Wilf Charles,
founder editor of 'Grey Power',
whose support for the first edition
ensured its publication*

Dave Goodman

FOREWORD TO 1998 EDITION

by Jack Jones

Dave Goodman's splendid book is indispensable reading for all who should know (or want to know) about the background to the National Insurance Pension. The publication of a new edition is an indication of the widespread interest the earlier edition aroused. It is hoped to reach an even wider readership at a time when the future of retirement pensions is very much in the news.

The early pioneer campaigners for an 'old age pension', whose story is recorded here, strove for a great principle over many years, eventually achieving partial success which blazed the trail for later improvements. It was indeed the forerunner of the present State Retirement Pension. Today that pension is secured by National Insurance through the contributions of workers and employers. This is the living contract between the generations, the younger paying their tribute to the older generation who laid the basis for the wealth of modern times.

We have to defend that principle against the new moves to replace it with 'every man for himself' philosophy. We need to strengthen National Insurance extending its cover to all, especially to women and carers whose work is inadequately rewarded, and improve its value. Unfortunately, that value has been undermined since 1980, and the spirit of persistence, determination and a sense of purpose of the early campaigners should inspire us all to press ever more strongly for policies of collective security in old age.

National Pensioners Convention President, Jack Jones, presenting a one and a half million signature petition at Buckingham Palace, 1996

In the words of Major Clem Attlee — Prime Minister of the Government which followed the ending of the Second World War in 1945 — 'we must combine together to meet contingencies with which we cannot cope as individual citizens — pooling the nation's resources and paying the bill collectively.'

The lesson of Dave Goodman's commendable work needs to be learned and applied, namely that determined activity in a good cause eventually brings success. I hope readers will see it as a call to action.

INTRODUCTION

The Act which first provided old age pensions in Britain was passed in 1908. It's 80th Anniversary, in 1988, is an opportunity to look back and learn from the story of how this milestone of progress was achieved. It is a story not to be found in the history books. These have little to say on the subject. Mostly they credit David Lloyd George with responsibility for the pension. The facts show this to be a travesty of the truth.

The reason that Lloyd George's name is linked to the pension is because he became Chancellor of the Exchequer in 1908. In that capacity he shepherded the Bill through Parliament, although it was introduced there by Mr Asquith following his elevation from Chancellor to Prime Minister. The fact that in 1908 an Old Age Pension Bill was introduced into Parliament was little thanks to Mr Asquith and none at all to Lloyd George. It was above all due to the ten-year battle which by then could no longer be resisted by the Government of the day.

The story of that battle is told in some detail because historians have shamefully neglected to tell it and it deserves to be remembered now and in the future. It is a story rich in lessons for today.

The same forces which 80 years ago were callously indifferent to the plight of the old are still with us and working hard to turn back the clock of progress. If past gains are to be held and further progress made, we cannot afford to forget the lessons of the past.

The battle for the old age pension was won by the combined forces of organised labour, religion and philanthropy. Its unsung heroes are Francis Herbert Stead and Frederick Rogers, Secretary and Organiser, respectively, of the National Committee of Organised Labour (the National Pensioners Committee). They were the outstanding leaders of a model campaign which eventually forced the Government to concede the pension. Many others played prominent parts, and their names feature in the following pages.

Of these, Charles Booth and George Cadbury deserve a special mention.

It is also of the greatest interest to see how the campaign for the pension was the main plank in the TUC initiative which resulted in the creation of the Parliamentary Labour Party. This, in turn, played a crucial role in overcoming resistance within Parliament to introducing pensions legislation. Without the mass pressure generated throughout the country, and a strong supportive force within Parliament, the breakthrough could not have been achieved.

Today, the organised Labour movement should be immeasurably stronger than it was 80 years ago. Today also, there is a powerful Pensioners' Movement which did not then exist. If these, together with all who care about social justice, are prepared to unite and show as much determination and skill as it took to win the pension, then the future well-being of the old can be guaranteed.

George Cadbury
Industrialist, Quaker and reformer

To this end I offer the following account, drawn mainly from contemporary sources, and in particular the work of the Reverend Francis Herbert Stead who is the authoritative chronicler of the battle he initiated and did so much to see, through good times and bad, to a decisive breakthrough. His book, *How Old Age Pensions Began To Be* (Methuen 1910), is the only full account of the campaign and is the basis of what follows.

Dave Goodman, 1988

POSTSCRIPT (For 1998 Edition)

The first edition of *No Thanks to Lloyd George* appeared about half-way through the 18 years of Thatcher and Major Governments. This one has come out during the second year of Blair's New Labour Government. In opposition, Tony Blair and his top colleagues condemned in no uncertain terms the Tories' betrayal of present and future pensioners. They now have the opportunity to return to the principles which guided organised labour 100 years ago in their pioneering struggle for the state old age pension.

Rather than sitting back and waiting for that to happen, all those concerned about the right to dignity and independence in retirement should be helping to make it happen. A hundred years ago Keir Hardie said, *Parliament does not respond to argument. It responds to pressure.* It is my hope that the story told here will encourage readers to lobby MPs and the Government. Labour's Election Manifesto commits this Government to maintain the basic state pension as the foundation for retirement. Yet so long as its annual uprating is linked only to the price index the basic pension cannot be a firm foundation for retirement. It lost about a third of its value, relative to earnings, between 1980 and 1997. That is one measure of the Tory betrayal condemned by Labour prior to the General Election. This year's annual uprating was the first test of Labour's determination to deliver its Manifesto pledge to pensioners. Sadly it failed that test with the result that 1998 saw the basic pension fall still further behind the level of average earnings. The state retirement pension is one of Labour's proudest achievements. Ninety years on the lessons of the past can ensure success for the campaign to defend and build on the achievements of the pioneers.

Before And After The Introduction Of Old Age Pensions

Before

In 1903 Will Crooks won a parliamentary by-election in Woolwich and became a Labour MP. As a child he had experience of living in a workhouse. His biographer, George Haw, tells the story:

The mother had been forced to ask for parish relief. For a time the guardians paid her two or three shillings a week and gave her a little bread. Suddenly these scanty supplies were stopped. The mother was told to come before the Board and bring her children.

Six of them, clinging timidly to her skirt, were taken into the terrible presence. The chairman singled out Will, then eight years of age, and, pointing his finger at him, remarked solemnly: 'It's time this boy was getting his own living.' 'He is at work, sir', was the mother's timid apology. 'He gets up at a quarter to five every morning and goes round with the milkman for sixpence (2½p) a week.' 'Can't he earn more than that?' 'Well, sir, the milkman says he's a very willing boy and always punctual, but he's so little he doesn't think he can pay him more than sixpence yet'.

The Guardians, firm in their resolve not to renew the out-relief, offered to take the children into the workhouse. The mother said 'No' at first, marching them all bravely home again. Stern want forced her to yield at last.

After such an experience it is not surprising that Will grew up as a bitter opponent of the treatment inflicted on those in need, especially the aged poor. He tells the story of a fine-looking old woman seeking poor relief.

She is scrupulously clean but poorly clad. The guardians' chairman says: 'Now, my good woman, what can we do for you?' 'Well, sir, we've nothing left in the world, and I've come to see if you can assist us.' 'Where's your husband?' 'He's ill in bed today. He's turned 73. I'm 75 myself. We've been living on the club money till now. He had six months full pay and six months half pay. That's as much as the club allows. Now we've got nothing. He worked up to a little more than a year ago. At 73 he can't work any longer. ' 'We are very sorry,' says the chairman, 'but the Poor Law practice is to ask old people like you to come into the workhouse' (which would have meant them being separated). 'Anything but that, sir,' pleads the old lady tearfully. 'Both of us over 70: we should feel it so much after working all our lives. We can look after ourselves if you can give us a little help'.

To escape the workhouse such people sold their furniture and anything else of value, acquired during a lifetime of hard work, but were often finally driven to the 'House'.

After

Often, 'ave we thought as 'ow it would be best for us to go, and sometimes almost 'ave I prayed to be took; for we was only a burden to our children as kept us; for they be good and wouldn't let us go on the parish so long as they could help it. But now we want to go on livin' for ever, 'cos we gives 'em the ten shillings a week, and it pays 'em to 'ave us along with them. I never thought we should be able to pay the boy back for all 'is goodness to me and the missus; but times change, sir.

(Husband of old couple over 90 interviewed by journalist, 1912)

THE DAYS OF NO HOPE

It is only in the 20th century that the old age pension has been a fact of life in Britain. The Act of Parliament which introduced it received the Royal Assent on 1st August 1908. Payment of the actual pension started in January 1909. Eighty years and three or four generations later the old age pension has become so much a part of the social fabric that it is taken for granted. It is hard to imagine that in Britain today there are people who were born before the pension existed. Even harder is it to understand the difference brought about by its introduction. Yet at the time it was clear that a social transformation would be the result of what to us might look like a very modest measure of social reform. At first the pensionable age was 70. Although payment did not depend on contributions it was subject to a number of conditions. It was means tested and paid according to a sliding scale. Maximum benefit was 5/- (i.e. 25p) per week and this reduced in 1/- (5p) stages according to 'yearly means'. If these exceeded the princely sum of £31-10-0 no pension was payable.

To appreciate the far-reaching consequences of this historic measure we have to look back to what it meant to be old in the days before the pension. This is movingly described by the man who, as Hon Secretary to the National Pensions Committee, played a large part in getting the Act onto the Statute Book, though only after a very long and bitter struggle which had to overcome powerful opposition. He is Rev Francis Herbert Stead, Warden of Browning Hall, a religious settlement in Walworth, south-east London. The driving force of his determination, and that of all who joined in the crusade for the pension, was their knowledge of the tragedy of 'want and age'. He tells of men who, after serving the same firm for over 20 years, were cast on the scrap heap at a week's notice when considered 'too old'. There followed a frantic and fruitless search for another job. Demoralisation and despair was the result and destitution the prospect. Some would go to live with, and become a burden on, a son or a daughter. If the burden became unbearable the victims in desperation were driven to applying for charity. Charity was sparing and it was cold. Those seeking it were subject to a pitiless inquisition about their past. At the end of this ordeal help was often refused because of some long-gone fault in early life.

Some men past work persisted in trying to work. Men who trembled for very age hawked trifles in the streets, tottering on through mud and sleet and icy winds. *Only those who have seen it,* writes Herbert Stead, *can conceive the misery of the poor old fellow who finds that society no longer has any use for him.* Manly old men came to him, tears running down their cheeks, seeking work . . . *Anything, no matter what it is, to keep me from the workhouse.* What kind of people were they who thus sought to escape the dreaded workhouse? Not thriftless, we are assured, but thoroughly respectable, sober, honest, thrifty and hard-working. God-fearing men and women who had brought up families but who in old age found themselves destitute.

He saw how the moment someone ceased to be of value as an economic tool they were flung aside as worthless. Age, far from being shown respect, was despised and rejected. In place of dignity there was the misery and humiliation of the workhouse. The workhouse was the last resort, its gate loathed more than the gate of hell. Self-respecting men and women driven into it by utter want died of very shame, their hearts broken by the degradation. Some, rather than go into the workhouse, simply starved until they died, the truth emerging at an inquest where evidence was given of their refusal to go into 'the House'.

Such was the fate of the aged poor. It had attracted some public attention. In the General Election of 1885 a lot was said about old age pensions, but nothing came of the talk. Ten years later a Royal Commission reported that a committee of experts was considering the possibilities of old age pensions. Three years later, in 1898, this committee, presided over by Lord Rothschild, presented its report. Its conclusions were grim and barren of proposals. The committee estimated that the population contained two million people aged 65 or over, of which two-thirds were in want, that is, 1,330,000 men and women. For them there was no word of hope. This is what these experts said: *We have been forced to the conclusion that none of the schemes submitted to us would attain the objects which the Government had in view, and that we are ourselves unable, after repeated attempts, to devise any proposal free from grave inherent disadvantages.*

These conclusions were accepted by the Government, and now that the experts had pronounced that nothing could be done it seemed that old age pensions were no longer on the agenda of public debate.

A GLEAM FROM DOWN UNDER

A surprising turn of events very soon resurrected the issue. While the mother country of the British Empire was slamming the door against old age pensions, one of its colonies, New Zealand, was passing legislation to introduce them there: 7/- (35p) a week at 65, means tested. When news of this reached Britain a ray of hope pierced the gloom cast by the 'experts' committee. The Warden of the Browning Settlement knew the London Agent-General of New Zealand, the Hon William Pember Reeves, and invited him to speak at the Settlement. A meeting was arranged for 20th November 1898, at which the new developments in New Zealand would be explained. From that small beginning can be traced the campaign which, though it took ten long years, finally succeeded in convincing the mother country to emulate, if less generously, the example of its daughter colony down under.

The announcement for the meeting simply said:

> **Old Age Pensions**
> **SEVEN SHILLINGS A WEEK**
> **After 65 years of age**
> **HOW NEW ZEALAND DOES IT**
> **will be explained by . . . etc, etc**

The effect was electric. Four hundred working people crammed into the hall at a meeting which can be fairly claimed to be historic. One who sent apologies for being unable to attend, but who subsequently played a key role in the campaign, was Mr Charles Booth, a Liverpool ship owner and the organiser of pioneering research on a massive scale into the extent and causes of poverty in London.

In organising the meeting Herbert Stead thought of it as a one-off event, not the start of a campaign. It was a member of the audience who approached him after the meeting to say, on behalf of several who were present at it, that they hoped the enthusiasm generated would not be allowed just to evaporate. Out of this approach came the suggestion of a conference, to be addressed by Charles Booth, to promote in Britain the cause of an old age pension on similar lines to that in New Zealand. An invitation to speak was sent to Mr Booth who promptly accepted, and the conference was fixed for 13th December 1898.

As first visualised the conference was to be local in character and attended by representatives of trade unions and Friendly Societies. A hundred circulars were printed and after sending out the local invitations Rev Stead found there were some left over. These he sent to Labour friends in different parts of the country, purely for information. To his intense astonishment he received acceptances from Bristol, Hull, Leicester, Manchester, Leeds and Newcastle, all from leading officials of major trade unions. He later said: *The casual despatch of those few spare circulars was the means of transforming the meeting from a local to a national conference, and that, too, one of unusual weight.*

There were less than 40 at the conference, though they represented a quarter of a million trade unionists. The birth of the Labour Party lay in the future and at this time the trade unions were the principal advocates of Labour's cause. They were by no means of one mind on many matters and exhibited the left, right and other differences of opinion we know so well today. All the clashing standpoints were present at this conference, itself an achievement, but even more remarkable was the total unanimity that emerged after the views of Charles Booth had been presented and discussed. Not content with this, the proposal was then put that similar conferences be organised in the main industrial centres of the country, all to be addressed by Charles Booth. At first he declined on the grounds of other pressing commitments, but such was the mood that he promised to sleep on the proposal before finally deciding. Next day he gave his agreement, thus paving the way for the next stage in the campaign. Conferences were planned at Newcastle for Northumberland and Durham, Leeds for Yorkshire, Manchester for Lancashire, and Birmingham for the Midlands.

Rev Stead had agreed to undertake the initial organisation of the four conferences. Thomas Burt, MP, a Northumberland miner who was one of the first two trade unionists to be elected to parliament in 1874, agreed to chair the Northumberland and Durham conference. Similarly, prominent personalities sponsored the other conferences, George Cadbury being the key figure for the Midlands conference.

THE MOVEMENT BEGINS

The gathering momentum of the movement is shown by how soon the first of the conferences took place. It was in Newcastle on 17th January 1899, just a month after the original conference, and that despite Christmas and New Year falling in between. Newcastle was regarded as a test case because Northumberland and Durham was a region noted for rugged individualism and an aversion to state intervention, even amongst trade unionists. The conference was held in Burt Hall, headquarters of the Northumberland miners. There were present 57 representatives from 37 trade unions, 29 from 20 Co-operative Societies and three from two Trades Councils, plus a number of visitors.

The Right Honourable Charles Booth, Privy Councillor

Charles Booth's address received an attentive hearing, followed by thoughtful discussion. The outcome was astonishing and totally unexpected. The 100 delegates, noted for their strongly held differences of opinion, found themselves in entire support of Mr Booth's argument. They voted unanimously in favour of a universal and non-contributory pension to be funded by general taxation, and a committee was appointed to further the movement in the two counties. It had been agreed that the conference would be prepared without the glare of press publicity, but a full summary of the proceedings was circulated by the newly-formed committee to branches of supporting organisations. The spectacular success of the Newcastle conference gave a great boost to the national campaign.

The Leeds conference came next, a month later on 23rd February. Besides the Yorkshire trade union movement, which was fully represented, there were delegates from Co-operative and Friendly Societies. The mood of this conference was very different. A few years earlier, in Bradford, the Independent Labour Party, led by Keir Hardie, had been formed and socialist ideas had gained ground in the trade union movement in Yorkshire. This was reflected in the conference discussion following Charles Booth's address. Some argued that unemployment was a more important issue than pensions; others saw the issue of pensions as a diversion from the need to bring about a social revolution. Yet, after Herbert Stead replied to the discussion, conference rallied to the need for agreement on essentials, differences to be shelved. Once again unanimity was registered in support of the claim for state provision of non-contributory pensions for all aged persons. Again, a committee was formed to carry forward the campaign, and press publicity was given to the conference, a sign of growing confidence.

The Lancashire conference followed two days later at the offices of the Co-operative Wholesale Society in Manchester. Twenty-six Trades Councils, 12 trade unions, eight Co-operative and three Friendly Societies were represented. This time the discussion had a distinctive Lancashire flavour followed by a unanimous vote in support of the proposals outlined by Charles Booth.

Requests now came in from Bristol and Glasgow to be added to the list of conference venues, and Mr Booth agreed. The Bristol conference on 11th March saw a representative West Country gathering as in previous conferences, but with some additional bodies including the Bristol Board of Guardians. Some opposition was anticipated but again Charles Booth's address converted all doubters — except one. When the vote was taken one hand went up against the pension proposition, this being the solitary opposing vote in the whole series of seven conferences. Its effect was to emphasise rather than detract from the overwhelming unity everywhere displayed.

The Glasgow conference drew between 200 and 300 representatives of the Scottish trade union movement, members of the city council and professors from the university. The debate following Charles Booth's address was lively, with conflicting views on how to fund the proposed pension, but once again the vote in support of state pensions was unanimous. Delegates were also elected to represent Scotland on the national committee.

This left only the Midlands conference to complete the series. By this time the impact of the previous conferences on public opinion was growing. They had, after Newcastle, been open to the press and widely reported. Printed notes, based on Charles Booth's address, had been circulated to stimulate discussion. Increasingly, old age pensions became a burning issue of the day. This was the background to the Midlands conference due in Birmingham on 25th March. Between two and three thousand invitations went out to organisations in the Midlands counties. Such was the response that the Lord Mayor's offer of the council chamber had to be declined in favour of a larger hall.

Amongst prominent individuals who received invitations was Joseph Chamberlain, formerly Lord Mayor and uncrowned king of Birmingham. Now the Colonial Secretary in Lord Salisbury's Government, he was still immensely influential in the Midlands. He sent an apology for being unable to attend the conference but expressed great interest in its proceedings. Without waiting for them he intervened in Parliament to make an important announcement of Government policy on pensions, namely that a Select Committee was to be appointed to consider the question again. He added that it was not a party political issue but one which should concern the best men of all parties. Even more significantly, he rejected the negative conclusions of the Rothschild Committee and expressed support for the non-contributory principle (a change from his former position). He balked, however, at the idea of a universal system of pensions, mainly on the grounds of its 'enormous cost'. Mr Chamberlain's views were endorsed by the opposition. So, thanks to the campaign, which had snowballed from a seemingly insignificant local meeting into a crusade of national proportions, old age pensions were now back on the political agenda.

Against this background the Midlands conference was held on 25th March in the large and beautiful Examination Hall of the City

Technical School. The room, which accommodated 700, was crowded almost to suffocation. As before, it was a delegate assembly representing the trade union movement, Co-operative and Friendly Societies. On the platform were prominent figures from the city's civic and philanthropic life. Due to the death of his brother a few days previously, George Cadbury, who had done so much to ensure its success, was unable to preside at the conference. He sent a letter urging, as a matter of duty for a Christian nation, better provision for the aged poor. Advocating the adoption of some measure like the New Zealand Act, he called on Friendly Societies and trade unions to agree on some definite pension scheme and to make it a test question at the next General Election.

With the added boost of the previous week's events in Parliament, Charles Booth's address was given a great reception. In the ensuing discussion he was challenged on the issue of universality, that is, his refusal to discriminate between the poor and the rich (the 'deserving' and the 'undeserving'). In reply he cited the parallel of free education, open alike to rich and poor, and he insisted that universality alone would remove the pauper taint from pension provision. The question of how to fund pension provision again occasioned some controversy, but the whole tenor of the conference became one of concern to bring about some practical achievement and not to be sidetracked from the main objective. Finally, a resolution was submitted declaring 'general and hearty support' to the principles set forth by Charles Booth. This resolution, printed in the agenda paper and in everybody's hands, was carried with absolute unanimity.

This marked the climax of that stage of the campaign inaugurated by the London conference. There had now been seven conferences which together showed an unmistakable depth of feeling about the need for Government action to provide for those we know as senior citizens. The agitation had some novel features. Its inspiration owed much to the shining example of New Zealand, a small colony which mocked the Imperial Government's excuses for inaction. Charles Booth, the key speaker at all the conferences, was no orator, so the progress of the movement was not based on rousing crowds with rhetorical exhortation but rather by the force of logical argument. Although it was inevitable in such a path-breaking and pioneering venture into social reform that there would be differences on some aspects of the proposals, so great was the desire for practical achievement that reservations were not allowed to impede the accelerating momentum of the agitation. Equally notable is the fact that, though parliamentary legislation was the objective, the movement was not in the hands of politicians. Said Rev Stead: *the nucleus of organisation is not the party caucus but the Trades Council or trade union. The professional politician recedes before the Labour leader. The philanthropist shoulders the task which the Cabinet minister has apparently dropped in despair.*

THE NATIONAL COMMITTEE IS BORN

Mr Chamberlain's promised Select Committee was set up on 25th April 1899. It consisted of 17 MPs whose job was *to consider and report upon the best means of improving the conditions of the aged deserving poor and for providing for those of them who are help-less and infirm.* This fell far short of the objectives of Charles Booth's proposals which had been so impressively supported throughout the country. Although Mr Chamberlain expressed the hope that, before leaving office, the Government would found a scheme *the experience of which will be extremely useful in the future and will lead to the ultimate solution of the question,* this may have been intended as a sop to the mounting pressure rather than as a seriously meant commitment. Any Government measure to provide a pension would require the prior agreement of the Chan-cellor of the Exchequer, in this case Sir Michael Hicks-Beach, later

Viscount St Alwyn. When he was no longer Chancellor he revealed that he had always believed that any old age pension was, on grounds of finance, impossible!

The national campaign was not lulled into inactivity either by the Select Committee or the Government's optimistic noises. On 1st May (Labour Day) 1899, Charles Booth published, in booklet form, a scheme of old age pensions which, for the first time, went beyond the general principles he had advocated till then. His book dealt first with the facts which highlighted the condition of the aged poor. The inescapable conclusion was that action on their behalf was long overdue. What form that action should take made up the book's second part. While recognising that there was a case for pensions at 65, or even 60, his scheme was based on 70 as the qualifying age. As for the amount of pension he considered various figures that had been mooted, before himself proposing 7/- weekly for a man and 5/- for a woman. This is just to give the bare bones of his detailed proposals. To see how they were received we have to look at the follow-up to the seven conferences.

At each of these a committee was formed to advance the movement. These seven committees combined to form a National Committee. This was quite large but from it a smaller executive was chosen. The new body had a long name reflecting its composition and purpose. The abbreviated form was The National Committee of Organised Labour, though it was widely referred to as The National Pensions Committee. One of its first decisions was that when the pensions were won they should be paid by the Post Office. They discussed what should be the qualifying age. Mr Booth's book said 70. An amendment proposed 60 but that was defeated. 65 was then put forward and agreed as the campaign objective. As for the amount of pension, Mr Booth's 7/- for men and 5/- for women was turned down in favour of 5/- for both men and women. It was also agreed that the cost should be met by general taxation. The Committee then decided to appoint a full-time paid organiser. In reaching that decision they were helped by offers from George Cadbury and Charles Booth to pay £50 per year each towards the cost. In this way the work of the conferences was carried forward, with a new organisation equipped to lead a nation-wide campaign.

The National Pensions Committee had the advantage of a climate of public opinion which, unlike that which followed the Rothschild Committee findings, was sympathetic to its goal. The Government, too, was pledged to legislate before leaving office in the quite near future. The National Committee, as a matter of urgency, therefore set about mobilising public support for the expected legislation to embody its main demands.

First to respond was the Congregational Union of England and Wales. Its Assembly unanimously carried a resolution in favour of *the widespread demand which is being made for old age pensions.* Charles Booth then published, for mass sale at the nominal price of one (pre-decimal) penny, a pamphlet, *Pensions for All in Old Age.* This outlined his general argument together with the National Committee's demands and list of members. He presented several thousand to the Committee for distribution. Then there was a succession of leaflets (which Rev Stead described as *the small arms ammunition of a campaign*). The first, *The Case Briefly Stated,* was composed by George Barnes, National Secretary of the Amalgamated Society of Engineers, and 100,000 were printed. George Cadbury presented 5000 copies of a full report of the proceedings of the Birmingham conference for free distribution. Added to these was the force of the spoken word. Union leaders involved in the campaign were taking part in meetings, public and private, all the time, and used every opportunity to argue the case for the pension. The Committee's notepaper carried this heading:

A free state pension for everyone on reaching 65 years of age. National committee of organised labour appointed at the seven conferences of Mr Charles Booth, with representatives of trade unions, Friendly Societies and Cooperative Societies.

The offer of Browning Hall to provide office accommodation was accepted, so the religious settlement which hosted the first purely local meeting now became the headquarters of a mighty national movement.

ENTER FREDERICK ROGERS

The first task facing the new National Committee was to find the right person to appoint as full-time paid organiser. It was a job that would call for very special qualities in view of the diversity of views and attitudes united in the Committee only on the pensions issue. A candidate acceptable to all was forthcoming, Mr Frederick Rogers, leader of a small trade union (the Vellum Binders). The optimists thought seven months would be

Frederick Rogers

enough to finish the job, while the less sanguine thought two years might be needed. It was decided to appoint him for one year, the engagement being annually renewable. There could not have been a better choice. He was at home in every circle, whether Hyde Park demonstrations, Conciliation Board, workmen's club, trade union, journalistic gathering, university common room, Deanery drawing room, or monastic retreat. What was the background of this remarkable man who was to play such a key role in a struggle even longer than the pessimists anticipated?

His origins were very humble. Born in Whitechapel in 1846 he began work as an errand boy to an ironmonger at 2/- (10p) a week. From childhood he suffered from spinal disease and this was aggravated by the heavy loads he had to carry. He became so seriously ill that he was not expected to survive. After treatment from several doctors which brought no improvement, at the age of 16 he was recommended to Dr John Watkins from whose treatment he greatly benefited. A relationship developed between doctor and patient and when the doctor's eyesight began to fail he asked the boy to read to him on Sunday mornings. This he did for four years and in the process developed his own literary and cultural interests. During this time he left ironmongery to learn the trade of vellum binding, but — in an age when free libraries did not exist — his interests extended to the insides of the books he bound. When 26 he joined the Vellum Binders Union and soon became an officer. The following year he joined the Stationers' Friendly Society and soon became an officer of that, too. He became a member of a School Board Management Committee responsible for four schools in Bethnal Green. For three years he was president of the East London Workmen's Club. From its earliest days he was an ardent supporter of the University Extension Movement which pioneered adult education, and in it he held important offices. He later joined the Co-operative movement and helped to found the Co-operative Bookbinders' Society. The trade unions, Co-operative Societies and Friendly Societies made up the three great groups of organised labour and his experience extended to all three. He also developed as a lecturer and began to write for the press, contributing many articles on labour questions. One of them, written in 1885, outlined a scheme for the formation of a Parliamentary Labour Party 20 years before its actual birth. His writing included, amongst other things, short stories for magazines. He became, in 1886, vice-president of the Elizabethan Society, and a lecturer in literature at Toynbee Hall. Turning down the offer of a well paid appointment as lecturer for the newly formed Unionist Party (which opposed Irish Home Rule and became part of the Conservative Party), he took the post of journeyman binder at the London Co-operative Society instead. After two years he became a foreman and it was that position he relinquished to join the National Committee as its full time organiser. Much more could be said about the varied and distinguished career of Frederick Rogers but it was notable that in every endeavour to which he applied himself there had been positive and worthwhile results. Now he faced his greatest challenge.

Confident that there would be early legislation and anxious to influence what it would decide, the new organiser went energetically to work. Circulars were sent to trade union organisations at all levels, and also to Co-operatives and Friendly Societies, inviting affiliation and subscriptions. It was made clear that this was not a party political enterprise, this being written into the constitution of the National Committee. To mobilise support a leaflet, *Hints for a Helper*, was distributed in 5000 copies. The following extracts illustrate the approach:

> *First of all get to know what is being done to push the pension movement . . . in your district. Our organising secretary, if you write to him, will be glad to give you this information, and to put you in touch with friends of the movement in your circle or neighbourhood. Then begin with organised labour. In your own trade union . . . warmly support any resolution enforcing our demand which may come from the headquarters. If the first step has not been thus suggested, take the initiative yourself. See that every member of your branch has a copy of our leaflet,* **The Case Briefly Stated** *. . . Get members to buy*

a copy of the penny pamphlet by Mr Charles Booth,
Pensions For All in Old Age *. . . our organising secretary
will supply copies as required.*

*Personally approach every official and every member of
much influence, and especially everyone likely to oppose
or misunderstand the movement. Ply them with printed
matter and personal persuasion . . . Then if, as our
experience leads us to expect, the general feeling is
favourable, submit to a regular meeting our circular
inviting affiliation . . . See that any decision to affiliate is
reported to our organising secretary, to the local Trades
Council, to the local MPs and to the secretary of your
national union.*

*In your Friendly Societies take similar steps . . . So with
your Co-operative Society. To win over the Trades Council
see the secretary, president and other leading officials
personally . . . You will now have formed a local knot of
members of Trade, Friendly and Co-operative Societies
who are ready to act together in furtherance of our
movement.*

*Approach public bodies . . . If you think the Board of
Guardians likely to yield a strong vote in our favour, get
an able guardian to move your resolution. Wait upon the
editors of the most influential newspapers of any party . . .
Lay on their consciences the sad plight of more than a
million aged poor.*

*Invoke religious bodies. In the name of the poor and them
that labour and are heavy laden, wait upon ecclesiastical
leaders such as the chief local dignitary of the Roman
Catholic Church, of the Church of England, and of the
dissenting bodies. Wait also upon the most numerously
attended and the most influential preachers of any
persuasion, and ask them to direct the attention of their*

congregations to the duty of making better national provision for the aged. Wait in the same way upon every important religious gathering, such as the Diocesan Council and the Free Church council . . . Work through the PSA (Pleasant Sunday Afternoon) federation, and the association of Adult Schools, to secure expressions of sympathy with our demand . . .

Caution! Keep yourself carefully from entangling alliances with any political parties. Our demand is not a partisan one. It is supported by men of different parties, and our movement must be colour blind to party distinctions. Our appeal is to 'good men in all parties'.

So long as this is clearly understood there can be no harm in plying local MPs and parliamentary candidates with questions, arguments and information; or in approaching local party leaders; or in addressing party meetings.

Get up local facts. Collect all useful information on the problem of old age in your neighbourhood.

Whenever you begin to feel tired of working for our movement, just think what you would do to save one poor old friend, your father or mother maybe, from the shame of the workhouse, from the inquisition of Bumble, or the ignominy of private 'charity'. You would not mind putting yourself seriously about for the sake of that one person. Then remember that in this movement you are working to save not one, but at least one million old men and women from such a fate.

GOVERNMENT PROPOSALS CONDEMNED

The Government's Select Committee on The Aged Deserving Poor, perhaps sensitive to the growing pressure of public opinion, completed its work just three months after its appointment, and on 26th July 1899, presented its report. What were its findings? Firstly, and most positively, *it is practicable to create a workable system of pensions for the United Kingdom* and *that the attempt should be made.* It then offered a system of its own. Here are the main points:

• A pension authority to be elected by the guardians in every Poor Law Union. (This recommendation would have made the administration of pensions the responsibility of those who administered the workhouses).

• Entitlement to pension would be subject to the following seven conditions. The man or woman must:

1) be a British subject;

2) have reached the age of 65;

3) have not within the last twenty years have been convicted of an offence and sentenced to penal servitude without the option of a fine;

4) had not received poor relief, other than medical relief, . . . during 20 years prior to the application for a pension;

5) be resident within the district of the pension authority;

6) have not an income from any source of more than ten shillings (50p) a week; and

7) have endeavoured to the best of their ability and industry, or by the exercise of reasonable providence, to make provision for themselves and those immediately dependent.

• The amount of the pension would not be less than 5/- (25p) and not more than 7/- (35p) a week, to be determined by the pension authority according to the local cost of living.

•The pension would be paid through the Post Office.

• The cost of the scheme, it proposed, would be divided between the funds of the Poor Law Union and the Government.

This report was sold out within hours of publication and had to be twice reprinted. It would be fair to say that it went down with the the campaigners like the proverbial lead balloon. The views of the National Committee's Executive, published on 23rd September, made the following main points: The appearance of the report was welcomed as a sign of progress on the pensions question during the last year. It contrasted the negative conclusions of the Rothschild Committee with the report's findings that pensions were practicable and should be introduced, together with an actual scheme for adoption. This remarkable change in the Government position it explained mainly as the result of the action taken by the working classes themselves following the seven conferences and the formation of the National Committee of Organised Labour.

It went on to say that, *while recognising a great stride forward has been taken towards our goal . . . the recommendations fall far short of what the situation required.* There followed a detailed criticism of the proposals, beginning with the attempt to distinguish between 'deserving' and 'undeserving' which would subject applicants to the gaze of the Poor Law inquisitors. The proposed machinery for administering pensions was condemned, especially its close connection with the Poor Law guardians. The disqualification of all with an income over 10 shillings per week was opposed, and it concluded: *The difficulties in which the proposals are involved only throw into greater clearness the simplicity, justice and feasibility of our demand for a free state pension for everyone on attaining a given age.*

The extent to which the pensions movement had taken hold of the world of organised labour was seen at the annual gathering of the Trades Union Congress held in Plymouth in September 1899. This was the first time that the Parliament of Labour had assembled since the formation of the National Committee. In its deliberations pensions were much in evidence, and a resolution was carried with total unanimity which echoed the sentiments of the National Committee outlined above. The resolution declared that. . . *no scheme dealing with old age pensions will be satisfactory to the whole of the workers in the country which makes it a condition of thrift or disregards the inability of a large proportion of the industrious and deserving poor to make provision for the future.* It favoured 60 as the qualifying age and ended with an instruction to the TUC's Parliamentary Committee (the forerunner of today's General Council) to *take such steps to make this question one of such prominence as to become one of the most pressing subjects at the next parliamentary election.*

That same Plymouth Congress also decided to bring together all sections of the working class movement with the objective of achieving distinctive Labour representation in Parliament at a time when the Conservative and Liberal parties monopolised Parliament. That initiative bore fruit in 1906 when the General Election returned 29 Labour members to Parliament and the Labour Party was born. It is interesting to record that the pensions campaign, which at the seven conferences found common ground among varying and sometimes conflicting elements in the trade union movement, is credited as a significant factor in creating the impulse to unity which found expression at the Plymouth TUC and the subsequent emergence of the Labour Party.

The forces of organised religion were rallied to add their support to the pensions campaign. Already the Congregational Union had taken this step. The Wesleyan Conference and Baptist Union were approached with good results. At the Catholic Congress at the end of July 1899, Cardinal Vaughan described the plight of the poor and expressed the hope that *the old age pension scheme might bring at least some remedy for this state of things . . . The well-to-do were afraid of its cost, but surely the rich were bound to tax themselves, or to be taxed, for their poorer brethren.* Support from the Anglican Church was sought next, leading to an invitation to the organising secretary, Mr Rogers, to address the London

Session of the Church Congress on 13th October. He spoke at a mass meeting in the Albert Hall and aroused the audience to great enthusiasm.

GREAT EXPECTATIONS SHATTERED BY BOER WAR

Thus far the national campaign had succeeded beyond the most sanguine expectations in rousing the conscience of the nation in general, and the forces of organised labour, philanthropy and the churches, in particular. It now seemed certain that the Government would, in the year ahead, 1900, introduce an Old Age Pensions Bill.

Then came an event that dramatically changed the situation. On 11th October 1899, the Boer War began. Overnight the National Pensions Committee found that the climate of opinion was transformed. The needs of the aged were no less, the remedy widely agreed, and the case which had received so much support was not challenged. Now, however, it was the war that claimed attention while demands for social reform had to take a back seat. Publicity for the pensions campaign disappeared from the press which was dominated by what was happening 'at the front' and by stories of 'battle, murder and sudden death' which came from South Africa. Nobody questioned the colossal expenditure on the war, though the very much smaller cost of introducing pensions had been seen as a grave problem.

Disheartening though the situation now was for the National Committee, it was not deterred and went on with its work. It gave a lead to existing local committees and established new ones. The commitment of organised labour to the cause of pensions continued despite the war. Frederick Rogers redoubled his efforts. He travelled the country speaking to all who would listen — an area conference of trade unionists, a working men's debating club, a lecture in an out-of-the-way colliery village or rural hamlet. He spread the gospel far and wide. Other members of the committee also refused to be deafened by the beating of the war drums and carried on the campaign. Charles Booth addressed a large meeting in Sheffield, with the Deputy Lord Mayor in the chair, and was supported by prominent figures nationally and in Yorkshire.

Early in the New Year 1900, the Government's Departmental Committee which was appointed to estimate the cost of the limited pension scheme of the Select Committee, issued its report. It estimated that in 1901 there would be over two million of the population aged 65 or over. It then deducted those with incomes of more than 10/- a week, a total of 741,000. Paupers were further deducted, another 515,000. Then 'aliens, criminals and lunatics', another 32,000. A further 72,700 were deducted 'for inability to comply with the thrift test', bringing the grand total of deductions to 1,360,000. This left only 655,000 as eligible for the pension, and the cost of it was estimated at a little over £10 million. What, with the cost of the war, another £10 million for their limited scheme was out of the question! What hope then, for the universal scheme demanded by the National Committee?

Facing now an uphill struggle in the new war-time situation, the National Committee refused to be daunted. It quickly brought out a manifesto, signed by 40 prominent representatives of labour organisations, which stressed the urgency of the demand for pensions. It was published in full, with all the names attached, in *The Times* on 25th January 1900 and made a strong impression. Two days later the Archbishop of Canterbury received a strong delegation of labour leaders and Rev Stead at Lambeth Palace, an unprecedented event. The deputation was rewarded by the Archbishop's whole-hearted support on a scale they could not have anticipated. He strongly supported pensions for all in old age and not just the 'deserving'. While recognising that the cost would provoke opposition, his answer to it was to fight the Chancellor of the Exchequer and to be very persistent. He concluded by saying that if the matter reached the House of Lords, *I should be very ready to defend very strongly what is now being sought by you, and to give it my vote.* Three days later hopes which had been rising were dashed. The Queen's Speech, which should have announced an Old Age Pensions Bill, curtly declared: *The time is not propitious for any domestic reform which involves a large expenditure.*

Clearly, a long haul now faced the National Committee but the struggle went on. In February 1900, as a follow-up to the TUC resolution mentioned above, the Labour Representation Committee was born. It brought together trade unions with labour, socialist and co-operative organisations seeking the return to Parliament of MPs not elected as Liberals or Conservatives representing labour. After one year its affiliated membership numbered 375,000 and for its first chairman the choice fell on Frederick Rogers, organising secretary of the National Pensions Committee. Scotland had its own Trade Union Congress and its support for the pension cause was next to be sought. In April Frederick Rogers went to its conference at Edinburgh and, though not a delegate, was given special permission to speak. Congress decided unanimously *that the time has come for the Government to bring in a bill to further a system of old age pensions.* Next the committee turned to the Co-operative movement and Frederick Rogers went to Cardiff on 5th June 1900 where he won the support of the Co-operative Congress.

From its inception the campaign had been intensive and sustained. Now, in July, came the first annual meeting of the National Committee. This was seen as an occasion to review the position and prospects they then faced. The Hon Secretary, Rev Stead, presented a survey which well conveys the blend of realism and determination which animated their continuing efforts. He began by quoting a remark recently made to him by a friend: *The war will have knocked the bottom out of your old age pensions movement.* On this he commented that the opinion expressed was common but mistaken, though conceding that the war had undoubtedly slackened the pace of the movement. Yet its effects were not wholly negative. It had deepened the sense of national unity and this could be turned towards a more responsible attitude to the condition of the aged population. On the question of expenditure the point was made that millions of pounds were being freely spent on behalf of a few thousand Outlanders (of British origin) in South Africa to ensure that they would not be deprived by the Boers of their right to vote. Yet at home thousands of old people, when forced to resort to parish relief, were robbed of their right to vote. The experience of the war also showed that the nation could sustain vastly increased expenditure without bankruptcy, if the will was there, thereby knocking out the old argument against pensions, 'that we can't afford the outlay.' Another factor was that the colonies had come to the help of the mother country in time of war; in so doing it brought home their shining example in the field of pension provision.

At the same time he faced reality: *Foreign affairs and military questions do threaten to overshadow the demands of home legislation for some considerable time to come. This is a fact to be sincerely deplored. But the balance will right itself in time, and internal reform must have its innings. Then that will be the time for enacting pensions.* When that time came he saw pensions and housing as the priority issues, in that order. *To have got the question into this unrivalled prominence is to have registered no small advance. Our own demand for universal pensions has made remarkable headway during the most exciting period of the war. Other and rival projects have retired or been abandoned. We . . . have been advancing our lines . . . under cover of the darkness; and when the day returns, our position and our strength will be an unexpected revelation to many.*

THE GREAT CAMPAIGN GOES ON

It became clear that sometime in 1900 there would be a General Election, even though in far-off South Africa the war was still raging. It was also clear that the war was the central issue that would dominate the election, thrusting social reform, including pensions, into the background. Meantime there was an indication, small but significant, of the impact on policy caused by the pensions movement. On 4th August the Local Government Board sent out a circular to Boards of Guardians ordering that the aged and deserving poor should receive *different treatment from those whose previous habits and character have not been satisfactory.* As no more substantial concession could be expected it was a case of being thankful, but not satisfied, for small mercies. Thought was now given to the role which the National Committee could play in the forthcoming election. All supporters were asked to use whatever influence they could muster to ensure the selection, regardless of party, of candidates committed to the pensions scheme:

> *Endeavour to get a PLAIN and STRAIGHT answer to the question 'Will you, if returned to Parliament, vote for a measure embodying the principle that every British subject in the United Kingdom shall, on attaining a given age, be entitled to receive a free pension from the state?'*

> *See that the widest publicity is given to the answer . . . Approach every editor, preacher, and important personage likely to exert influence . . . Only where a personal interview is impossible communicate by letter.*

> *Use our printed matter freely . . . Where it would help our movement, heckle candidates publicly on the question. REMEMBER, over a million old folks, in workhouses or dishonouring indigence outside, are depending on your*

action in this general election for speedy or for tardy release from their present degradation. See to it that their release shall be speedy!

200,000 copies of a manifesto entitled *Old Age Pensions For All: An Appeal To The Electors* were printed. This went fully into the case of the National Committee. A shorter statement was also felt necessary and Mr Rogers drew up a concise little leaflet, *The Worn-Out Workman: What Is To Be Done With Him?* Every member of both Houses of Parliament was made acquainted with the objects and work of the campaign. Mr Rogers summed it up: *In preparation for the general election, 200,000 copies of* An Appeal To The Electors, *500,000 copies of* The Worn-Out Workman *as a handbill, and 5000 copies of the same as a poster, and 1000 copies of a special poster for agricultural districts were printed . . . Letters were sent to 50 of the leading newspapers in the United Kingdom . . . and two days after the letters appeared the general election was announced.*

The election campaign itself lasted little more than a fortnight, from 25th September to 13th October, but an intensive effort was made to utilise the printed materials to the best advantage. During that period Frederick Rogers visited Leeds, Sunderland, Newcastle, Romford, Southend, Walthamstow, Woking and Enfield to help forward the drive. The Committee saw all this effort as an educational activity, not a campaign for seats. There was, however, one seat contested simply and solely on the question of universal old age pensions. The candidate was Councillor Stevens, the chairman of the National Committee. He stood as an Independent and his platform was the demand for pensions as a civil right. The seat he contested, East Birmingham, was in the heartland of Joseph Chamberlain, the Colonial Secretary. Councillor Stevens' chances of winning were nil, especially during the war, but he polled 2835 votes against 4989 for his opponent, Sir J B Stone. The effort was not in vain. At a time when ministers concentrated wholly on war issues, and none more than the Colonial Secretary, Mr Chamberlain was compelled to speak about pensions at a constituency public meeting. *We have not done with old age pensions*, he said. *The tale is not quite told yet. Perhaps if he (Councillor Stevens) will give me time, I will be more fortunate than I have been in the past.*

The outcome of the election was another Conservative Government with an overwhelming majority in both Houses. It was opposed to universal pensions but pledged up to the hilt to some form of pensions legislation at some, unspecified, future time. This was the prevailing situation which now confronted the National Committee. The war was expected to be soon over (but did not come to the end until 1902). There was no lull in the campaign. Every newly-elected MP was sent a report on its work by the Committee, with a request for their opinions on the pensions issue. The many replies received were revealing. Much sympathy was expressed but only limited commitment. Younger MPs of both parties were more helpful than their respective elders.

There can be few campaigns in history which sustained the kind of momentum kept up by the pensions movement in the face of circumstances so clearly discouraging. Not only was there the negative impact of the war on all issues of social improvement. There was also a newly elected Government from which little or nothing could be expected. At the very best its approach to pensions fell far short of the policy advocated by the National Committee. Hope deferred, it is said, makes the heart sick. That did not apply to the hearts of those campaigning for justice to be done to the old. With remarkable dedication, energy and persistence the battle continued to create such support from public opinion that no Government would be able to hold out against it. That objective was held in view during the long, hard years ahead until victory was achieved. Today's pensioners owe a debt that should always be remembered to those who pioneered that momentous breakthrough that was to change millions of future lives. Understanding how they did it will help us today to repay that debt by ensuring that no Government is allowed to turn back the clock and again make old age a time of needless suffering, humiliation and premature death.

PROGRESS AGAINST THE ODDS

In the difficult situation which followed the general election the National Committee still saw its task as pressing for the earliest possible pensions legislation. All MPs were sent campaign material and asked for their view, as we have noted. A sign of the influence of the campaign was seen at a Conservative national conference on 18th December when a resolution was moved which criticised the Government for its failure *to introduce a measure for the solution of the problem of dealing with the question of old age.* The mover, Mr H S Foster, was not thinking only of the old, for he referred to many good friends of his in rural areas who, as a result of the Government's failure *had lost their seats on that one question alone.* Such evidence helped to fuel the continuing agitation and a brief look at how it was conducted is of interest.

Heading the organisation were the two guiding figures, Francis Herbert Stead and Frederick Rogers. They had regular meetings, twice or more weekly, to monitor progress and consider new ideas and suggestions. This was backed by frequent meetings of committees, sub-committees and officers, characterised by a degree of informality making for action based on consensus. In all this work a great contribution was made by the only woman on the National Committee, Miss Margaret Bondfield of the Shop Assistant's Union (and later a Labour MP and the first woman to enter the Cabinet). To advance the cause nothing was too much trouble. Requests for speakers sometimes came from far-off, isolated, out-of-the-way places where the audience was likely to be small. Provided bare out-of-pocket expenses were paid, such requests were not turned down. A favourite platform was the PSA (Pleasant Sunday Afternoon, under church auspices). Adult Schools, Mutual Improvement Societies and club debates were catered for. Many public discussions, in which prominent public figures took part, were held. The message was carried into the universities and into the courses of the University Extensionists (pioneers of present-day adult education). Although the campaign was non-party, this did not mean ignoring the political parties, Quite the reverse; the aim was to win understanding and support from all parties. The power of the medium (singular in the days before radio and TV made it the media) was concentrated in the press, national and provincial. They provided invaluable publicity, with a generally constructive response to the activities of the pensions movement. Even the small rural papers which lacked prestige but did reach the agricultural labourer were not despised, and helped some backsliding Conservative MPs to lose their seats.

It was not the press that most influenced public opinion but the leaflet, of which many were printed and distributed in great quantity. Personal correspondence, aimed at 'everyone of serious importance in any sphere of life', was organised, the correspondent being the particular secretary or member of committee with readiest access. Even more productive, though very time-consuming, was the personal interview. In the case of MPs, Herbert Stead's description vividly recalls the nature of this task: *To send in for MPs already bored with all manner of calls upon their attention and sympathy, and to wait their convenience or freedom from more absorbing engagements, is a dispiriting process and somewhat lowering to one's sense of dignity. But the conversation, however obtained, was generally worthwhile . . . And not infrequently the interview that had taken some trouble to obtain proved the beginning of a real personal friendship.*

Then there was help that was unsolicited. In 1900 Miss Isabel Faraday, a cousin of the great scientist Michael Faraday, presented the Browning Settlement with the house she formerly occupied, in East Dulwich, as a home for old folks. This was opened on 25th October 1901, followed by a public meeting at the Settlement at which Sir James Crichton Browne spoke on the work of Faraday. He also took occasion to refer to the anxiety caused by fears of a destitute old age. Were that fear removed by a pension, however small, but certain, the result would be an immense gain to the mental health of the nation, and so to its economic efficiency.

The response from many better-off public figures to this campaigning was two-fold, firstly an expression of the deepest sympathy and compassion for the suffering of the aged. Secondly that they could see no practical scheme which they could support to relieve that suffering. When they became convinced that the principles of Charles Booth's scheme were the only logical and proper ones for dealing with the problem they raised another obstacle. The nation would never consent to the cost of that scheme (willing as they were to support it), so nothing could be done!

Organised labour continued its solid support, especially the trade unions and particularly the Trades Councils (there was still no Labour Party). The Trades Councils represented trade unions on a local basis. Following the General Election a circular was sent to every Trades Council in the United Kingdom urging that they pass a resolution calling on the Government to legislate on old age pensions on the lines of National Committee policy, and to send copies to local MPs, to the Prime Minister and to the Leader of the House of Commons. Sixty-three of them reported having done so, and many others took action without reporting. It was a nationwide response from Inverness to Devonport, from Paisley to Dover, from Cardiff to Norwich, and nearly every great industrial centre in between. In the fight for the old age pension the National Committee awarded special battle honours to the Trades Councils.

Although much support had already been registered in Scotland it was felt that this could be substantially increased. Two conferences were organised — for the west and the east of Scotland. Both were resounding successes. Another triumph for the campaign was registered at the annual assembly of the Co-operative Congress which spoke in the name of ten million members. It unanimously carried a resolution which referred to . . .*the urgent necessity of parliament providing an old age pension for every citizen.* This consolidated and extended the support secured earlier in the year at Co-operative conferences.

MORE LIGHT FROM ABROAD

The old age pension as an issue was obtaining wider international currency. On the same day that the Co-operative Congress added its support for the campaign in Britain, a conference of the International Federation of Miners in London expressed its general support for provision of pensions for the old. Three weeks later an Old Age Pensions Bill was introduced into the French Chamber of Deputies. Then the lead of New Zealand bore fruit in Australia. The colony of New South Wales, in December 1900, passed an Old Age Pensions Act which, though providing for a means test, made 65 the age of eligibility and ten shillings (50p) the amount paid weekly. It went even further and entitled all incapacitated for work by physical disability, regardless of age, to the same pension. Then, a few days later, the sister colony of Victoria passed its Old Age Pensions Act, also applicable at 65, which provided a pension of 7/- (35p) weekly. Again there was an extension of provision, this time to all of any age who were permanently ill through unhealthy occupations. Twelve days later, 1st January 1901, the Australian Commonwealth was inaugurated and with it the prospect of further extending the legislation.

These stirring developments on the other side of the world were not without repercussions in the mother country. A meeting was arranged at Browning Hall on 20th January for Sir Andrew Clarke, Agent-General for the Colonies of Victoria and Tasmania to speak about the new Australian legislation. This he did, adding that in his opinion the only right thing was to give a pension to everyone reaching a certain age (he favoured 60), peer or peasant, without any exceptions; so that a recipient should feel it was not a dole or charity but a right which could be proudly accepted for services rendered to the state.

The National Committee wished to give public recognition to the great New Zealand initiative which had played such a vital part of the problem in Britain. Its treasurer, Mr Edward Cadbury, was due to visit New Zealand and it was decided that he should deliver an address to the Premier of New Zealand, the Rt Hon Richard Seddon. It began: *Will you permit those who are working in the United Kingdom for the amelioration of the condition of the aged poor to present an address of respectful congratulation to you, whose country has been the first state in the English-speaking world to create by law pensions for its aged citizens?* It went on later to add: *Your initiative has been followed by . . . the creation of the National Committee of Organised Labour as the direct result of your ideas working here.*

The address was signed by a distinguished list of 40 public figures from Parliament, local Government and the trade union movement. Among the MPs were Thomas Burt, John Burns, James Keir Hardie and Richard Bell; others included Will Thorne, James Ramsay MacDonald and Margaret Bondfield.

In his reply to the address the New Zealand Premier included the following prophesy: *The names of those . . . who are prominent in the struggle to bring old age pensions within the realm of practical politics in England are sufficient guarantee to all earnest souls that ultimate victory is assured.* Both the address and reply were given great prominence in the press.

There was no short cut to that ultimate victory. Formidable obstacles had to be overcome. Among them was the attitude of Joseph Chamberlain, Colonial Secretary, who was the key Government figure on the issue of pensions. He was opposed to universal pension provision which, according to him, the country couldn't afford and which would destroy independence and discourage thrift. He expressed these views at the Annual Conference of the National Order of Oddfellows (a leading Friendly Society) in Birmingham on 29th March 1901. He then advanced his own proposal, namely that by the aid of and through the organisation of Friendly Societies a scheme should be worked out in which, assisted by the state, a pension at a fixed age might be secured to those who had contributed towards it.

The National Committee saw Mr Chamberlain's intervention as a challenge. Their task now was to win the support of the Friendly Society movement for full support of its policy in the same way as it has won the support of the trade unions and the Co-operative movement. In this way the threat to universal provision, as distinct from a limited contributory scheme, would be defeated. A leaflet was drawn up, *Why We Should Not Subsidise The Friendly Societies To Get Old Age Pensions*, which trenchantly refuted the principle proposed by Mr Chamberlain. It demonstrated that Friendly Societies did not provide a mechanism adequate to the task, and that if they were endowed by the state as the instrument for pension provision the result would mean *taxing the ill-paid labourer to pension the well-paid artisan, taxing the weak to pension the strong, taxing women to pension men, taxing the many to give a privilege to a few.*

The facts which led to that conclusion were fully explained in the leaflet and can be briefly summarised. Total membership of Friendly Societies was some five million out of a national population of forty million. So Government funding for Friendly Societies, out of revenues to which the whole population contributed, would be unjust to seven-eighths of the population. Then, in general, it was the better paid wage earners who could afford Friendly Society membership. Why should the low paid be expected to subsidise them? Also many in poor health were not accepted as Society members. They would not benefit from Mr Chamberlain's scheme but would be taxed towards its cost. Amongst the low paid working women were worst paid of all and unable to afford the subscription to Friendly Societies, many of which excluded women from membership. So the leaflet made a powerful case for the rejection of Friendly Societies as the Government's chosen instrument to administer a limited and selective pension scheme. 100,000 copies of the leaflet were printed and widely circulated. They went to the press, which largely reprinted it; to every MP; to the clergy; to Friendly Society lodges; to all the campaign committees for local distribution; and were introduced into by-elections.

Towards the end of 1901 the Parliamentary Committee of the TUC tried to organise a triple conference where the forces of the trade unions, Co-operative and Friendly societies would be combined. In the event the Friendly Societies declined the invitation but a joint trade union — co-operative conference, with some individual Friendly Society participation, did take place on the 14th and 15th January 1902. This conference unanimously supported the policy of the National Committee, a step forward for the campaign. Then in March came the turn of the Friendly Societies whose national conference was due to meet in Manchester. Their response to Joseph Chamberlain would be specially significant. The outcome was the following resolution, carried by a majority of three to one: *That this conference, representing three and a half million members, is of the opinion that it is the duty of the state to provide an old age pension of not less than five shillings a week to all thrifty and deserving persons of 65 years of age and upwards who are unable to work, and in need of the same, and that such a scheme shall place no disability of citizenship upon the person claiming the pension, and that the cost of the same shall be raised without any interference with the funds of the thrift societies.*

This was a crushing rebuff to Mr Chamberlain (regarded as *the most powerful minister in the most powerful Government of modern times.*) Although the conference did not go all the way with National Committee policy its key importance was the rejection of the contributory principle, and its effect was to leave the proposals of the National Committee as the sole policy being pressed upon the Government with massive popular support.

END OF WAR RAISES NEW HOPES

This continuing effort by the National Committee and its supporters was taking place while the Boer War was still the dominating influence in public affairs. Then came the news, in June 1902, that the war was over. Now, they felt, was their opportunity. For a long time their cry had been After the War — Pensions! With peace at hand pensions must now be practical politics.

In this spirit the National Committee gathered on 24th June 1902, full of energy and determination. It was decided to press ahead with plans for a winter campaign. The aim of this was to ensure that the level of national taxation, now that there was no longer a war to pay for, should enable pensions for all to be provided the following year. It was planned to draw up a Bill to this effect for introduction into Parliament.

At the same time the Committee received the resignation of its Chairman, Councillor Stevens, who had served for the three years since its formation. Appreciation of his service was suitably expressed and George Barnes was invited to succeed him. He, too, had been in from the beginning. George Barnes occupied a position of influence in public life. When only 13 years of age he began an engineering apprenticeship in London which he completed in Dundee five years later. From the age of 18, as a time-served engineer, he followed his trade for 15 years in Scotland, Lancashire and London. Throughout this time he was an active trade unionist and became well known in his union, the Amalgamated Society of Engineers. In 1892 he was appointed to a post in the union's head office. After three years there he went back to work at his trade. Two years later, in 1897, he was elected to the proud position of General Secretary. At that time the Amalgamated Society of Engineers organised 100,000 skilled and well-paid workmen who occupied a key position in the industrial life of Britain. It was one of the strongest unions in the world. Since leaving school at 13 Mr Barnes had made good his lack of formal education by wide reading, travel and participation in public life. He later entered Parliament where he was able to render special services to the pensions movement of which he had now became National Chairman.

By happy coincidence a Colonial Conference was then taking place in London. Amongst the overseas Premiers attending was the Rt Hon Richard Seddon from New Zealand who had sent such a stirring reply to the National Committee's Address. He now accepted an invitation to speak at Browning Hall on how the great pioneering pensions experiment was working out in practice in New Zealand. The meeting, crowded and enthusiastic, took place on July 30th 1902. The New Zealand Prime Minister was careful to insist that he could not interfere in the domestic affairs of Britain, and no resolution could be put. He declared that old age pensions were a question of humanity and he was carrying out the wishes of New Zealand pensioners in making their system known. His people would be glad if they could come to the help of the aged in the mother country just as they had sent their sons to defend the empire on the battlefields of South Africa.

He described the situation in New Zealand, the numbers involved of total population and those eligible for pensions, which included Maoris, and the cost, which was borne by general taxation. There had been bitter opposition to overcome before the Act was achieved. He himself had been kept at the table of their Parliament for 187 hours defending it. Then he turned to the situation in Britain. Could it, he asked, bear the burden of old age pensions? If they had known that when the Boer War began it would cost £260 million they would have been horrified. Yet they were able to bear that burden. To introduce universal pensions it had been calculated would cost some £8 million a year. He was certain that money could be found. When the honour of the nation, and justice to the aged poor was concerned, the question was beyond any consideration of money sacrifice. As an old Oddfellow he ridiculed the idea that any man or woman would be thriftless simply because at some future day he or she might receive a pension of 5/- a week. Besides, the poor must be kept. The question was to a large extent one of relieving local rates and transferring the cost to general taxation. No one doubted they must succour helpless infancy; there was equal if not greater claim to assist indigent old age. He believed that a country that did its duty in these questions of humanity would be blessed. New Zealand had prospered, and was now more prosperous than ever. At the last election not a single candidate had proposed the repeal of the Act.

This inspiring address was followed by a notable proposal from Charles Booth, who chaired the meeting. He raised the battle cry — *Pensions before remission of taxation!* — heralding a campaign which resounded through the country for ten long months of resolute struggle.

This campaign was based on a manifesto headed: *To The Working People Of Great Britain And Ireland — Why Not Pensions In 1903?*

It followed the lines indicated above and began: *We have got the money for them now. The present revenue can bear the cost. The taxes now flowing into the treasury are sufficient to supply, over and above the ordinary expenditure, a free pension for every aged person in the United Kingdom. Taxation has been forced up for the war. It must be kept up for pensions.* It recognised that the Government would only give way if faced with overwhelming mass pressure, because there were rival claims on the surplus revenue. *Unless still greater pressure is exerted in favour of pensions, the Government will yield to the rival claims and we shall have missed the great opportunity of securing pensions for all without imposing one penny of additional taxation.* It went on with practical guidance for raising the level of the agitation throughout the country. Put pensions before party, it appealed. The watchword must be: *Pensions first — remission of taxes later!*

The campaign had much to contend with. The mood which followed the end of the war was one looking for relief from taxation. To pay for the war the Government had put seven (pre-decimal) pence in the pound on income tax; and levied duties of three pence on a cwt of corn, 50 pence a cwt on refined sugar plus an export duty of a shilling a ton of coal. Coal owners and miners, general consumers and taxpayers, were all hostile to the continuation of the wartime burdens to fund a pension scheme.

The National Committee had every confidence that there was overwhelming support amongst working people for its policy of pensions first, remission of taxes later. Its problem was to demonstrate that support and turn it into a political force to which the Government would have to respond.

A lead was given by the 1902 conference of the TUC held in London. This again unanimously affirmed its demand for universal pensions. The committees all over the country were mobilised. To highlight the new drive it was decided to open the London campaign at Browning Hall where the movement was born. The PSA Brotherhood went to work in the Borough of Southwark with the aim of holding a town's meeting. Handbills were distributed from door to door, street by street, with women in the forefront. Rev Stead paid tribute to them: *Anyone who thought of the working womanhood at the base of the social scale as a sodden, dull, inert mass of unintelligence would have had a wholesome surprise if he had seen the enthusiasm of these Southwark women. They were the first at the doors, more than an hour before the meeting began.*

The night of the meeting, 20th October, was wet and dismal but still the hall, holding 2000, was crowded. The Mayor presided and almost all local leaders spoke or wrote in support of the demand. A resolution, moved by George Barnes, was put to the meeting: *That the enactment of old age pensions should precede any substantial reduction of taxation.* This was strongly supported by a number of MPs and church dignitaries, including Dr Bourne, then Roman Catholic Bishop of Southwark and later Archbishop of Westminster. This enthusiastic gathering gave the winter campaign a magnificent send-off. Next came a leaflet — *A Four Years' Fight for Old Age Pensions as a Civil Right: a diary of the progress of the movement from despair to the brink of attainment.* The Southwark resolution was soon after supported at large meetings in Brixton, Hampstead and Poplar, in London, and other towns in the country.

At this time 23 prominent labour leaders, who would have had much to contribute to the campaign, were serving in America on the Mosely Commission. From Niagara Falls on 19th November 1902 they declared their solidarity with the efforts being made back home. They signed a manifesto which called for legislation on old age pensions to precede any substantial reduction of taxation, and concluded: . . . *though absent from England we would urge on our fellows to relax no effort to support the agitation which aims to make pensions for the aged become the law of the land.*

PRESSING ON DESPITE BREAKDOWN

As a result of overwork Frederick Rogers completely broke down and went to Cornwall to recover his health, but the winter campaign went ahead. Expressing strong opposition to the efforts of the National Committee was the Charity Organisation Society. Their work, doling out charity only to those who could prove themselves worthy, would be undermined by pensions for all.

Anyone looking at the actual policy of the National Committee would be struck by the contrast between its moderate terms and the fierceness of the many sided opponents who were able for so long to frustrate its implementation. Those moderate terms were embodied in *A Bill to Provide Pensions for the Aged* (as approved by the National Committee of Organised Labour, 7th February 1903). This was unanimously adopted by the Committee after careful clause-by-clause consideration, and was presented as a focal point for the campaign.

The Bill called for a pension of 5/- weekly to be paid to every British subject, male or female, from the age of 65 except those

(a) domiciled outside the UK;

(b) born outside the UK and with under 20 years' UK residence prior to application;

(c) under police surveillance;

(d) who on conviction of crime have been sentenced to deprivation of pension.

Also included in the Bill was provision for the pension to be paid at the nearest post office. It further provided that pensions would be forfeit during terms of imprisonment being served, or if courts specified a period of loss of pension as a penalty. It also provided that any pensioner becoming an inmate of a workhouse would have the pension paid to the Guardians of the Poor for the duration of their stay. The Bill, hopefully, declared that the operative date of its implementation should be 1st October 1903.

It will be seen that there was nothing reckless or extravagant in the policy of those battling for the pension, but the opposition remained determined to prevent the Bill ever reaching the statute book. Nevertheless the drafting of the Bill did furnish a platform to which supporters could rally. First to do so were a number of MPs — John Burns, Thomas Burt, Charles Fenwick, John Wilson, Richard Bell and D Shackleton.

Having won the argument in the country the National Committee concentrated its efforts on the House of Commons. This was the Parliament returned in 1900 after a 'Khaki Election' while the Boer War was still raging. It was not naturally responsive to appeals for social reform. There was as yet no Labour Party and the two traditional parties — Conservative and Liberal — were both indifferent to the call of social justice for the old. It was this unpromising assembly which now was to be tackled.

Towards the end of 1902 every MP was sent printed campaign material and asked to reply to the following two questions:

1) Will you vote for the enactment of old age pensions prior to any substantial reduction of taxation?

2) Will you vote for a Bill to make a free pension from the state the civil right of every aged person who is not disqualified by crime or recent alien origin?

Out of 630 members there were 47 replies: 22 said yes to both questions; 10 said no; the remainder sat firmly on the fence. A by-product of the exercise was a lot of good publicity in the press, especially in the provincial press.

Despite this, and firm support from the Irish MPs who then sat in the House of Commons, it proved impossible to make pensions an issue in that session of Parliament. Not a word about pensions appeared in the King's Speech, even though the Government was committed to doing something about them. Parliamentary procedure was used to block the introduction by a private member of the National Committee's Bill. Other initiatives were stalled by members who, while pledged to support the pensions issue, gave higher priority to other issues. The whole experience was a poor and depressing return for those who had devoted so much effort to rousing Parliament to the urgency of immediate action to alleviate the plight of the old.

WILL CROOKS ENTERS THE HOUSE

The prevailing gloom was lightened by the return to Parliament on 11th March of Will Crooks, elected with a large majority as member for Woolwich. He was, in his own lifetime, a legendary character, having risen from being an orphan workhouse boy to being a London County Councillor and now an MP. From its very inception he had been an active stalwart of the National Committee, and in the Woolwich election he made pensions a major issue. His opponent declared that *thriftlessness and want of backbone are the chief causes of destitution of the working classes in old age*, adding roundly that *working men do not want pensions*. This provoked an intervention by the National Committee which signed a manifesto calling on the electors, of all parties, to vote for *Crooks and justice for the aged.* After his election by 8687 votes to 5458, Will Crooks declared that the result was *an overwhelming mandate for old age pensions.* His commitment to that mandate, as an MP, was never in doubt.

Will Crooks MP

The budget of April 23rd 1903 did nothing for the old, even though the Chancellor had a surplus of £10 million (a very large sum then) at his disposal. Fourpence in the £ was taken off income tax, thus making a present of £10 million to the middle and upper classes. The National Committee registered its indignant protest. It said:

This is class legislation in its worst form; it is anti-national in its tendency, and is in direct violation of the promises of the last 10 years. it was the party now in power who told the nation that a better treatment of the aged poor was possible. The nation believed those words, and they have been miserably defrauded and deceived, and we still remain behind nearly every other nation in the civilised world in our clumsy and blundering efforts to solve this form of the poverty problem. The leaders of the opposition did not escape censure in this statement.

A further setback came just three days later when Joseph Chamberlain, the only Cabinet Minister with any interest in pensions, embarked on a new stage in his career. Henceforth he abandoned any concern with social reform and channelled all his energies and influence into leading an agitation for tariff reform. The ensuing controversy over free trade versus tariff reform became the dominating issue in the political arena, with pensions a casualty of that controversy.

Prior to the budget there had been a Second Reading debate on a Private Member's Bill. Mr Remnant's Aged Pensioners Bill aimed at granting discretion to the Boards of Guardians to give pensions of 5/- or 7/- weekly to deserving cases from the age of 65, to be paid for partly by the Treasury and partly from the rates. The National Committee found this measure defective. It limited pensions to the poor and deserving, linked them to the Poor Law, with ratepayers paying part of the cost. Its only value was as a peg on which to hang a debate. The debate was unproductive with speakers taking no notice of the available £10 million surplus. Will Crooks intervened to give notice of his intention to move on the Second Reading of the Finance Bill *that no Bill will meet with the approval of this House which does not provide for the appropriation of the surplus at the disposal of the Government to the claims of the aged poor before al other claims for relief.* This was ruled out of order on procedural grounds. When the Finance Bill was debated Will Crooks spoke, on the 9th June. He exposed the character of the budget and restated the case for giving priority to pensions, adding: *I regret that the rules of the House will not permit me to move the amendment I proposed to move.*

That was the end of the 'Pensions in 1903' agitation. Much hope and effort had been expended but the outcome was failure. The reasons for this failure were sought so that lessons could be learned.

The conclusion was drawn that for any breakthrough it would be necessary to look to a new House of Commons, and one containing more MPs of the character of Will Crooks.

FACING A CRISIS

The National Committee now faced a crisis. Up to now it had maintained a high state of morale in its uphill struggle which had won over key sections of public opinion. The climate of political debate moved adversely for it, and other issues were in the forefront, especially education, tariff reform and the financial aftermath of the war. Just how gloomy the situation was is shown in this letter from Sir Brampton Gurdon MP: *If ever old age pensions are given, they must practically be universal, and not simply good conduct prizes. But I am afraid I must adhere to what I said at the General Election — that the enormous cost of the war would render any scheme of old age pensions impossible during my lifetime. Any MP who, for the sake of popularity, encourages his constituents to believe that in face of the present heavy taxation and large accumulation of debt, it will be possible for any Government to take up the question during the present generation, will be pursuing a very dishonest course, as he cannot but be aware that he is promising what he cannot perform.*

People who had played an active part in the campaign decided it was time to drop out. Subscribers withdrew support. Trade union bodies were loath to part with hard-earned cash when no result could be foreseen. Personal contributors began to question the point of maintaining an organisation which had such little hope of success. With the approach of winter the financial outlook of the National Committee looked very bleak.

Crisis point was reached when a group of leading supporters of the Committee considered withdrawing their support. Had they done so the blow could well have been fatal. They approached Rev Stead, from whose initiatives the Committee had largely stemmed and of which he was Hon Secretary throughout. If he felt the work should go on they would not withdraw. He was in no doubt. Although having no illusions about the Parliament of the day his faith in popular support was unshaken. He still believed that the cause was practicable as well as just. The country could afford the proposed pension scheme. Also, the recently formed Labour Representation Committee was preparing for the next General Election, selecting candidates and constituencies. Those elected would be pledged in support of the Committee's policy. On these grounds he persuaded the waverers that they had a duty to carry on. From that time onward their loyal and wholehearted support was never in question. The campaign went on.

Frederick Rogers was back in harness and carrying through a heavy programme of meetings in town and country. He also took up the pen. A publisher began a series of **Pro and Con** books, beginning with old age pensions. The 'Pro' section was written by Rogers, the 'Con' case being put by Frederick Millar, secretary to the Liberty and Property Defence League. In reply to Mr Rogers' arguments for pensions legislation Mr Millar concluded: *To contend that persons who simply will not save and invest their savings for their own advantage should have their thriftlessness encouraged at the expense of the community is surely a proposal too unblushing in its effrontery to need further remark.* The book's publication gave a lift to the pensions case. It helped to publicise the 'Pro' case and expose the weakness of the opposition.

A significant advance was recorded in February 1904 at a conference of the Labour Representation Committee. Looking to the future it adopted a resolution which included an instruction to the Labour Party (not yet formed) *to draft and bring in a Bill to pension all men and women after the age of 60 years, the funds to meet same to be raised from the same source as the £250 million expended upon the late war in South Africa.* Thus old age pensions became the first plank of social reform in the platform of the yet unborn Labour Party. While encouraged by this, the National Committee continued to seek support from electors regardless of party.

While having no hope of legislation, efforts were made to make pensions an issue in the new session of Parliament which opened in February 1904 with a King's Speech which again had nothing to say on the subject. The budget in April showed an expected deficit of £3 million to meet which a penny was put on income tax and twopence on tea. Not a very helpful background but an opportunity was provided by the debate on another Private Member's Bill, the Aged Pensioner's Bill, on similar lines to that of the previous year and equally unacceptable to the National Committee.

The most revealing contribution to the debate was from Sir Michael Hicks-Beach, Chancellor 1895-1902, during which time early pensions legislation had been promised. He exposed the hypocrisy of that promise in a speech opposing the Second Reading of the Private Member's Bill. This included the forthright statement *I think this House ought to be honest. Do any of you believe it is possible for an old age pension scheme to become law?*

While Parliament was being reminded about the needs of the old, other steps were being taken to strengthen the agitation. Good press publicity was secured, and every opportunity at meetings and conferences to register renewed support. Frederick Rogers addressed a 4000-strong audience on the subject at a Church Congress, and later at an International Congress held in Edinburgh. The National Committee found itself faced with what we now call a 'cash flow' problem — not enough money coming in to finance the work needing to be done. Mr Rogers explained: *In March I found it necessary to bring our financial position before the Executive . . . our funds were low . . . and with the full consent of the chairman, vice chairman and sub-committee, I agreed to continue my office without salary for 12 months . . . using what funds we had for necessary work, such as printing, postage, etc . . . The work has been longer than we thought at first, but we have had loyal supporters and faithful friends, and if we all resolve to keep it steadily in the fore-*

front of politics, it is the one piece of constructive legislation before the country today, and we shall yet see the reward of our labours. He added that the principal hope of success at the parliamentary level rested with the Labour members. *I know they believe in this cause,* he said, *but they ought to fight for it better in the future than they have in the past.*

A FORWARD LOOKING STRATEGY

It was widely felt that the next General Election could not be long delayed. It was time for a new Parliament to succeed that elected in 1900 during the war now long over. Accordingly the campaign strategy was to influence public opinion to ensure that pensions figured high on the list of issues on which the next General Election would be fought.

At the end of August 1904 a leaflet was widely circulated: *Parliamentary Candidates and Old Age Pensions.* This leaflet was a practical guide to supporters, briefing them on how to heckle candidates. It identified three types of candidate:

1) Convinced supporters of the pensions proposals;

2) Honest opponents; and

3) Wobblers.

While encouraging steps to convert the honest opponents, it was the wobblers who were seen as the danger.

In the words of the leaflet: *In questioning a creature of this type on old age pensions there are certain stereotyped replies, largely supplied by the election agent, with which the 'heckler' must in no way be satisfied. Here is a sample of the kind of dialogue that can often take place between questioner and candidate:*

Q   Are you in favour of pensions for the aged in place of Poor Law relief?

A   I am willing to support any well considered scheme of pensions; or,

I am in favour of pensions provided they do not hinder the work of the Friendly Societies; or,

I am in favour of pensions for those thrifty and deserving; or,

I am in favour of some scheme of old age pensions, but have not yet seen one that satisfies me.

The reply to the first answer is that it is an evasion: there was a well-considered scheme, that of the National Committee of Organised Labour. Would he support that? The second answer is also an evasion and the candidate should be reminded that the National Committee of Friendly Societies was amongst the organisations on record in support of a universal pension scheme. The third answer required the 'thrifty' and 'deserving' concepts to be dealt with. The fourth was just not acceptable — the issue was too important for a non-committal attitude when ample literature was available from the National Committee.

Armed with this leaflet, supporters everywhere were well primed to put pressure on candidates of all parties.

In the run-up to the awaited General Election there were a number of by-elections. Both the Conservative and Liberal candidates were lobbied and according to their replies the National Committee either declared both to be satisfactory, or pronounced in favour of the more satisfactory of the two, regardless of party.

A by-election at Horsham, Sussex, produced a notable development. The Liberal candidate had promised full support but in the event back-tracked on his promises and tried to ignore the pensions issue. The Conservative candidate, who had made no promises, also ignored the issue. It so happened that Rev Stead rented a small cottage in the constituency and was therefore an elector. He drafted a manifesto *On Behalf Of The Aged Poor*, and canvassed the clergy in the constituency for support. His appeal was signed by no less than 32 ministers of religion — Anglican, Baptist, Roman Catholic, Congregational, Wesleyan, Primitive and Unitarian. The resulting publicity compelled both candidates to reply at length. Both local and national press gave major coverage to this exchange and the candidates' attempts to ignore the issue were foiled utterly.

It was strongly felt that the next General Election would be crucial, and this feeling dominated the work of the National Committee in 1905. The official policy of the two parties was to be non-committal about pensions, so the committee's efforts were directed to the rank-and-file of both. The Labour Representation Committee, which made pensions a priority issue, was gathering strength.

The trade unions, and especially Trades Councils, were still a major source of support, and to the latter Mr Rogers addressed a special message. In this the likely date of the General Election was seen as a year ahead, 12 months in which to build up the pressure. *Do not be misled*, it said, *by the false parrot cry, invented by the enemies of this reform — They can't afford it; they've got no money: it won't come in our time . . . What happens in our time depends entirely on the people of our time. They can have old age pensions now if they are determined to have them.* The message gave practical guidance on how to conduct the agitation.

THE VOICE OF THE AGED POOR

Amongst those touched by the pensions campaign were the old people whose needs gave rise to it. Their expectations were expressed in letters that poured in from all over the country. Publicity was given to them, of which this excerpt is an example illustrating the life story of an agricultural labourer:

I began working for a farmer in this neighbourhood at a penny a day, and work has been my lot ever since. I do not complain of it; indeed, I have had my happiest times when so engaged. I never got more than 2/6 (12½p) a day. I was married in 1863. I have had, and reared without parish relief, four children. They are all grown up and they are good members of society. My wife is beside me in this happy little home to this day. We live here, where we have lived for 25 years. The rent I pay is £6 a year, and all is straight up to this day. Now, after all these years, we feel the pressure of old age coming down upon us, and we fear what may be ours soon to know: how soon we know not. It seems so hard to have the parish pay hanging over you. I have always paid my way, and have even done the best I could to help my poorer neighbours in their trials, and thus have tried to do my best for my country and for all. I have the same feeling and desire now but my strength fails me, and I am conscious that the weakness of old age is upon me. Will you pardon me for thus writing to you? Believe me that I am not seeking my own good alone. I plead for thousands of my fellow men and women as well as ourselves. I feel that simple justice calls mightily for old age pensions for the people of England.'

Then there was the poor widow, 68 years old, who had reared four children and was now alone, who wrote: *The guardians will not allow me relief and tell me I am able to work. It is very hard and I fear I shall be driven to the workhouse.*

These are but two of the many cries from the heart which, with variations, told the same story of a life of useful toil ending with the dread prospect of the workhouse as the last home before a pauper's grave.

Despairing of any Government action Mr Rogers addressed an appeal, over the heads of ministers, to the King (Edward VII). This was published in the Morning Post and duly acknowledged by the Secretary of State. It was a long and moving letter which told of the plight of the old and expressed disillusion with Parliament — a graveyard of people's hopes littered with broken promises. *If the Great Assembly,* he wrote, *fails us — and it is failing us for all practical purposes — where shall we look for the voice which shall authoritatively declare the convictions of the nation?* So, he appealed to the monarch, quoting from a recent speech by George Barnes: *Old age pensioners were discussed in the reign of Edward VI (in the 16th century): I hope we may see the discussion come to fruition in the reign of our justly popular King Edward VII.* This hope was in fact realised, though not without further delay and stalling. Meantime the lobbying for support went on. Ireland was still part of the UK and sent MPs to Westminster where they made up a distinctive group, and it backed the pensions campaign. A new Archbishop of Canterbury was approached to reaffirm the positive attitude of his predecessor. This he did and valuable publicity resulted. More positively, the leader of the Nonconformist Churches circulated all Free Church candidates in support of the National Committee. When, in October 1905, a by-election took place in Hampstead these church leaders' views, together with those of Roman Catholic Cardinal Vaughan, were circulated as a leaflet amongst the electors.

The General Election could not be much longer delayed and its imminence spurred the local committees of the campaign to renewed action. So, both nationally and at local level, the work went ahead with added vigour and rising expectations.

A Historic General Election Creates A New Situation

At last the Government of Mr Balfour came to its end. He submitted his resignation and on 5th December Sir Henry Campbell-Bannerman became Prime Minister. The long-awaited General Election followed in January 1906, and its consequences were to prove momentous.

No-one had waited more impatiently for this trial of strength than the National Committee. It was well-prepared and issued its election manifesto just four days after Mr Balfour's resignation. It was an eloquent, but well-reasoned, cry for justice *for the worn-out worker, man or woman, who has helped to build the fabric of our national life and who demands not charity, but justice.* It was a cry that did not go unheard or unanswered by the electors.

This General Election ended a 20-year period of domination by the Conservative Party. The Liberal Party was swept into power with a landslide majority. This, however, did not guarantee the success of the pensions campaign. That depended on the new forces which now took their place in Parliament including 29 members Labour Representation Committee. Now, at last, the Labour Party came into being. This parliamentary upheaval was to prove highly significant for the outcome of the long battle for pensions.

Eleven members of the National Committee were amongst the newly elected members. Some were Labour, some Lib-Labs (that is, Labour members of the Liberal Party). Some were former members re-elected, but six of the 11 were altogether new to the House. Of these special mention must be made of George Barnes, Chairman of the National Committee. Amongst the others were leading members of the provincial committees of the campaign, such as Mr Wilkie, convenor of the Northumberland and Durham Committee and the first to propose the all-important series of conferences.

Another was Mr J R Clynes who chaired the first Manchester conference. In all, the Committee's MPs were broadly representative of the country. One of them, John Burns, had become a Cabinet minister; another, Thomas Burt, the Northumberland miner who had been an MP for over 30 years, was made a Privy Councillor.

Clearly, in this new Parliament the prospects for the campaign were transformed, which is not to say that victory would be won without a determined struggle. The newly-formed Labour Party adopted the device with which we are now familiar. It assigned responsibility for major policy issues to individual members, and so formed Labour's first 'shadow Cabinet'. The old age pensions portfolio was given to George Barnes.

A formidable task faced the fighters for pensions. The Liberal Party, with 380 MPs, had an overall majority of 134. It had no election commitment to old age pensions. As Mr Asquith, the first Chancellor of the new Government said at a later date: *His Majesty's Government came into power and went through the last General Election entirely unpledged in regard to this matter.* Though this was true of the Liberal Party as a whole, many individual Liberal MPs had pledged support for the policy of the National Committee in response to the campaign. It was subsequently estimated that around four-fifths of all the MPs in that Parliament had been won to express support. Still, the Government's reluctance remained an obstacle to be overcome.

First to raise the issue was a deputation from the Parliamentary Committee of the TUC to the Prime Minister, Sir Henry Campbell-Bannerman, and the Chancellor, Mr Asquith. Amongst several issues raised was the demand for a universal pension of 5/- weekly from the age of 60 funded by the Government. The Prime Minister was sympathetic. He agreed that a universal pensions scheme would not discourage thrift but would promote it. It was for the Chancellor to deal with the financial aspect. He, too, was sympathetic but could not see the way clear to finding the money. *For the moment,* he said, *I tell you frankly I do not possess it, and I have no reasonable expectation of possessing it.* That was the Liberal Chancellor's first word, two months after taking office; it proved not to be his last word.

The General Election of 1906 not only returned the Liberals with a landslide majority and enough Labour MPs to found the Parliamentary Labour Party. It also gave rise to a very different, and more purposeful, House of Commons. In matters of social reform the change of climate was described as being from Greenland to Queensland.

Australia once again gave a stimulus to the pension struggle in Britain. Soon after the new Parliament assembled at Westminster, there was published the report of the Australian Commonwealth Commission on Old Age Pensions. It rejected Friendly Societies as the medium for a scheme of pensions, and also the contributory basis. Its proposal was that *the Federal Government shall grant pensions of 10/- weekly as a legal right, not as a charity, to all persons of 65 years who have resided continuously in the Commonwealth for 25 years and whose annual income does not exceed £25.* In cases of permanent incapacity it would grant a pension at the age of 60. It was expected that these proposals would soon be implemented.

The new temper of the House was soon revealed. The King's Speech had again made no mention of pensions. In the debate on the Address George Barnes drew attention to this omission and declared the determination of the movement and of the Labour Party to rectify it. He was followed by Mr H W Lever, a leading captain of industry, who expressed general support for the case argued by George Barnes. That these representative voices of Labour and Capital should be in such agreement on the issue was seen as reflecting the strength of national feeling outside the House.

LABOUR PRESSURE COMPELS GOVERNMENT PROMISES

On 14th March, a month after the House had assembled, the Labour Party made pensions a priority issue in its parliamentary programme. It introduced a motion — *That in the opinion of this House a measure is urgently needed in order that out of funds provided by taxation provision can be made for the payment of a pension to all aged subjects of His Majesty in the United Kingdom.* The debate on this motion aroused intense interest and took place in a full House with the Visitor's Gallery crowded and many people turned away. The motion was moved by Mr J O'Grady, Labour member for East Leeds, and seconded by Mr Grove, Liberal MP for South Northants. Between them they made a powerful case, including the fact that on pensions this country lagged behind nearly every country in Europe.

Mr Asquith, the Chancellor, spoke for the Government. His speech reflected the new political climate, but also that there would be no victory without sustained struggle. He expressed the Government's willingness to accept the motion and the principle it embodied. Then came the 'but' — the Government's support was subject to finding a practicable means to give effect to the principle.

Before going on to discuss the cost, Mr Asquith declared that the two most tragic figures of the day were the man who wants work and cannot find it, and the man who is past work and has to beg for his bread and his bed. These, he said, constitute a standing reproach to our civilisation and a perpetual problem for statesmen. Then came the financial reckoning. He figured that the annual cost of a national pensions scheme would be somewhere between £13 and £26 million. How could this be raised? He pointed to reduced expenditure on the army and navy, and on education, together with measures to increase revenue from taxation. His conclusion was *I am not without hope . . . The Government hope, not*

65

at once, but gradually and I hope effectually, to make some progress towards the solution of this problem. Significantly, he went on to recognise the presence of a driving power such as they had never had before in the House of Commons. This new driving power was largely embodied in the new Parliamentary Labour Party, and its members were accorded great respect from the MPs of both traditional parties.

In the course of the discussion Mr Asquith committed the Government to a universal, i.e. non-contributory, scheme. John Burns, the long-time supporter of the National Committee, was now President of the Local Government Board and a member of the Cabinet. He fully supported *the universal scheme put forward by Mr Charles Booth, by which everybody was to receive a pension irrespective of conditions or means,* adding, *we must bring to bear upon the Government such efficient, reasonable, disciplined and well-organised pressure as would compel, or better still persuade, them to begin some form of old age pensions.*

The resolution, which affirmed the principle of pensions for all in old age, was carried without a division, with only one solitary 'No' against a thunder of 'Ayes'. It was a response which recalled that of the early launching conferences seven years earlier. It was a major landmark in the struggle through by no means the end of the road. It was one thing for the Government to be committed 'in principle'; quite another to turn that commitment into legislative practice. The National Committee was under no illusions on that score and lost no time in following up its success in Parliament. The aim now was to build up that persistent pressure referred to by John Burns. As a first step towards this a meeting of sympathetic MPs was called to consider ways and means. The invitation went out in the names of George Barnes, Will Crooks, Enoch Steadman and John Ward. The meeting was held in a House of Commons committee room with Rt Hon Thomas Burt in the chair. Those present included Labour MPs and some Liberal MPs. On other issues there were sharp differences but on pensions they were in agreement.

The outcome of the meeting was the demand, supported by all present, *that we demand an old age pensions from the Government next session.* It was further agreed to seek a private interview with the Chancellor to make representations on behalf of their views, these to be put by George Barnes, Chiozza Money and Mr Burt.

COUNTRYWIDE SURGE IN SUPPORT

The building up of pressure was not confined to Parliament or to London. On 5th May a great conference was held in Wakefield convened by the Yorkshire Federation of Trades Councils. Two hundred and eighty members of 154 trade unions and 66 delegates from 36 Co-operative Societies, representing 376,800 members, attended. The Bishop of Wakefield presided. He said only the Labour movement could drive home to the community the deplorable facts of age and poverty. These he regarded as a challenge to Christians and he called on all his brother clergy and ministers and all the favourably circumstanced to support the campaign. Keir Hardie, who later wrote of this as 'an inspiring week-end', told the conference it was time for Acts not pious demonstrations. The conference called unanimously for an Act without delay from the Government.

At that time the Congregational Church was closely allied to Liberal Party politics. If it could be mobilised, Congregational opinion would mean valuable pressure on the Government. This was duly expressed at the Congress of the Congregational Union held in May. The following resolution was moved by W H Lever MP, seconded by Hally Stewart MP, and carried unanimously: *That, in view of the election pledges of MPs, this Assembly urges upon His*

Majesty's Government to give legislative effect in the next session of Parliament to the resolution which the House of Commons has this year passed without a division, demanding pensions for His Majesty's aged subjects.

Three days later, on a Sunday evening, a vast open air meeting was held in Derby market place to further the cause. The chairman, a JP, said the gathering was fittingly taking place on the Sabbath Day since the effort to secure pensions for the aged was essentially Christian work. George Barnes MP drew attention to the fact that there already were 171,323 people drawing state pensions to the total tune of nearly £8 million. Mr Richard Bell, the local MP, urged that similar demonstrations be held in the population centres to force legislation on Parliament.

After more than two months' delay the deputation of three met the Chancellor. A meeting to report their discussions was arranged at the House of Commons on 21st June attended by MPs sympathetic to the campaign — 6 Liberals, 4 Lib-Labs and 8 Labour, together with the Hon Secretary and organiser. Thomas Burt gave a full report of the deputation's reception by the Chancellor. Mr Asquith had expressed his support for their ideas, but . . . ! The 'but' was the cost which he described as large. He could make no immediate commitment and would have to await the report of a Select Committee enquiring into proposals for graduated income tax. Only then could he decide whether to include a pension scheme in his next budget. To this report George Barnes added that the Chancellor was estimating the cost of a pension scheme as around £15 million, while Chiozza Money expressed confidence that the Select Committee report would lay the basis for greatly increased Government revenue. In this way the unanimity which had been a feature of the Committee from its beginning was preserved intact.

That still left the next step in the campaign to be decided, in order to raise its level both in the country and in Parliament. As to the latter it was agreed to ask the Prime Minister to receive a large deputation of MPs at the beginning of the autumn session. As for the country, the objective was to create a climate of opinion which would make for the success of the Parliamentary pressure. To the extent that its funds allowed the Committee arranged a programme of public meetings at each of which the demand was put forward for the next budget to include provision for the introduction of pensions. When, in July, the National Committee held its seventh annual meeting the mood was buoyant, a far cry from the earlier despondency. It was now felt that there had been remarkable progress and that the winter agitation would achieve results.

A flying start was given to the campaign with a delegate meeting at Rotherham on 1st September attended by 407 delegates representing 47,202 members from trade unions, Friendly Societies and Railway, Co-operative and Women's Guilds. Total support was registered for pensions legislation without delay. The press gave wide publicity to the event and its message was conveyed to the Government.

Two days later the TUC Annual Conference at Liverpool reaffirmed its eight-year long support dating back to the very beginning of the campaign. It unanimously adopted a resolution which instructed the Parliamentary Committee (of the TUC) to circularise all affiliated unions urging them, through their local branches, *to bring pressure on MPs and to use every other effort to ensure the passing of an Old Age Pensions Bill next year.* The implementation of this resolution after the conference reinforced the nationwide agitation for early legislation.

A MEMORABLE OCCASION!

When Parliament reassembled for the autumn session the Government was pressed to receive the Parliamentary deputation on the 20th November and this event became the focal point of the National Committee's efforts. It was a memorable occasion! The deputation, which met in the room of the Prime Minister, Sir Henry

Campbell-Bannerman, numbered nearly 80, all of whom, except Rev Stead and Mr Rogers, were MPs. Thomas Burt was the spokesman for the deputation. He traced the history of the movement back to the inaugural conferences of 1898-99 and featured the role of Charles Booth whose principles had been supported by all shades of organised labour. He ended by stressing the urgent need for early legislation.

One of the MPs present, Mr Theodore Taylor of Batley, speaking as a Liberal and as an employer, declared that pension provision was the responsibility of the state and that many employers shared that view. Some of the trade unionists present added their representations and the Prime Minister was left in no doubt as to the strength of feeling on the issue, both in the country and among MPs.

Replying to the deputation the Prime Minister said that he fully agreed with everything that had been said. Only two things stood in the way of conceding what the deputation was demanding — want of time and want of money. As for the scheme that should be legislated he accepted it should be universal and non-contributory. It would be legislated, he promised, as soon as time and money could be found. He was followed by the Chancellor, Mr Asquith, who began by agreeing with everything said by the Prime Minister. He expressed himself with great feeling and declared that no Chancellor with funds available would ever be so lacking in basic humanity as to refuse to come to the help of helpless age. Nothing lay nearer to his heart than the desire to introduce the scheme on which they all agreed. For the Government, he insisted, it was a question of extreme urgency.

The deputation departed feeling greatly encouraged though still without a definite promise to introduce an Old Age Pensions Bill in the next session of Parliament. Still, the Government had an overwhelming majority so 'extreme urgency' — if it was sincere — could only mean early legislation.

An official report of the interview was drawn up by George Barnes, leader of the deputation. It was submitted to, and approved by , the Prime Minister and then circulated to the press. This happened on the eighth anniversary of the speech by Mr Pember Reeves at Browning Hall which triggered off the movement, now seemingly in sight of victory. In fact there was still bitter disappointment to be faced and overcome by continuing determination and struggle.

Throughout the country the momentum of the campaign increased. One example is that of a Conference in Plymouth for the three towns of Plymouth, Stonehouse and Devonport that now make up that city. Held on 8th December, it brought together 208 delegates from religious, trade union, labour, Friendly Society and other organisations. Total support was expressed for the National Committee's policy.

Not unnaturally, expectations were now running high. Then on 12th February 1907 came the King's Speech for the new Parliamentary session. It promised nothing on pensions. In the face of this rebuff George Barnes moved, on behalf of the Labour Party, an expression of regret that the Government had not seen fit *to include amongst the measures promised for this session one making provision of an adequate pension for the aged poor.* His speech concentrated on the question of cost and showed that ample wealth was available for taxation. He pointed out that in 1900 nine men died leaving estates worth over £19 million, and that since 1900 forty-six had left over £78 million. The Labour Party, confident of an embarrassingly large anti-Government vote, determined to push the matter to a division.

In replying to the debate the Chancellor appeared to be conceding to pressure. He also had at his disposal a substantial surplus and there were precedents for introducing measures not mentioned in the Royal Address. Accordingly, in anticipation of a Pensions Bill during the session, the Labour and Lib-Lab MPs decided not to divide the House. Then John Burns, a former advocate of the National Committee policy but now a Cabinet minister, spoke in favour of further fact-finding and delay prior to legislation. Keir

Hardie promptly protested that this was an excuse for another 12 months' postponement instead of pensions in 1907 as the Chancellor's speech had implied. The decision not to divide the House, he said, would not have been taken if John Burns had spoken sooner but they would stand by it. Then the opposition pressed the matter to a division with 61 supporting the amendment, 213 the Government, and the rest — a majority of all Members — abstaining. It was a bitter reminder to the National Committee of the old saying: Put not your trust in Princes — or, in this case, Government Ministers.

SYMPATHY, PROMISES AND DELAY

Two months later, on 18th April, the Chancellor presented his budget to the House. He was in the happy position of having an estimated surplus of over £3 million, enough to make a pensions scheme possible. The subsequent contrast between his words and deeds is a classic example of the politician's art of procrastination. He repeated the Government's commitment to pensions: *This I do say, and I wish to say it with all the emphasis of which I am capable, speaking for the whole of my colleagues, that in the sphere of finance we regard this as the most serious and the most urgent of all the demands for social reform.* Yet his conclusion was an anti-climax: *It is our hope — I will go further and say that it is our intention, before the close of this Parliament — yes before the close of the next session of Parliament, if we are allowed to have our way — it is a large if — to lay firm the foundation of this reform.* Then, after a budget which benefited the already well-off, he talked about measures to build up a fund *for the relief of necessitous old age.* He estimated that next year, 1908, he would have in hand, *earmarked for the purpose,* £2½ million plus an additional sum from increased estate duties. So the old were left to wait and suffer while the Chancellor accumulated funds. When Rev Stead returned to Browning Hall after listening to Mr Asquith's speech in the House, he found a bevy of pressmen waiting. *What,* they asked, *was the verdict of the National Committee on the budget?* To which he replied that while welcoming the news that a pensions fund was being built up, they deeply regretted that the Liberal Government, like the previous Conservative Government, had put the comforts of the middle class before the bitter needs of the aged toilers.

The Government's promises did not dispose of the matter. In May 1907 Mr W H Lever introduced a Private Member's Bill. It proposed a three-stage introduction of pensions. In the first year 5/- to all over 75; in the second year to those over 70; and in the third year to those over 65. The cost to be met nine tenths from the exchequer and one tenth from local rates, and the scheme to be funded by graduated income tax. The Bill, accepted in principle by the Government, was read a second time but nothing further materialised.

What made a bigger impression on the Government was the shock result of a by-election at Jarrow caused by the death of a Liberal MP. A Labour candidate, Peter Curran, contested the seat and made pensions a major issue. The Liberal candidate got no help from Mr Asquith who stuck to the lines of his Budget speech. The result was a clear victory for Labour. Peter Curran's vote was 4,698 against Conservative 3,930, Liberal trailing third with 3,474, and Nationalist 2,122. Two weeks later the Government suffered an even heavier blow when the Colne Valley Division returned Victor Grayson (Socialist) ahead of both Liberal and Conservative opponents. This was a sensational result and was subjected to varying interpretations, though they all agreed it was a victory for the cause of old age pensions.

At the annual meeting of the National Committee held on 21st July, the main resolution included the following section: *It desires to call attention to the result of recent by-elections as a proof of the growing impatience of the working classes at this delay (of pensions legislation) and anticipates similar results in other working class constituencies unless official assurance is forthcoming that the first place in the legislative programme next year will be given to a measure providing pensions for all in old age.*

The autumn and winter of 1907 saw a very vigorous agitation in support of the demand for immediate legislation. Beginning with a great open air demonstration at Bristol on 30th August, the National Committee organised a large number of meetings throughout the country. For the eighth year in succession the TUC, at its annual conference, affirmed its support for the campaign and instructed its Parliamentary Committee to hold a series of meetings. These were held in Manchester, Leeds, Dundee, Birmingham, Newport (Mon), Newcastle-on-Tyne, London and Dublin in November and December 1907 and January 1908. The Labour Representation Committee, which in 1906 became the Labour Party, held its eighth annual meeting in January and called on the MPs to conduct an agitation on pensions throughout the country. In Yorkshire the Federation of Trades and Labour Councils organised a petition, appealing for support to trade unions and trades councils, Co-operative and Friendly Societies. 799,750 signatures were obtained and Mr F Jowett MP presented the petition to Parliament. It urged immediate action and stressed that Britain was a wealthy nation well able to afford the cost of the proposed pension scheme. Ireland, then part of the United Kingdom, weighed in with enthusiastic demonstrations in Dublin and Belfast. Prominent public figures also added their voice to the swelling movement, amongst them George Bernard Shaw then enjoying great acclaim as a successful dramatist. He replied to a letter in the Westminster Gazette and trenchantly refuted the suggestion in which he detected *marks of official inspiration* that any pension scheme should be means-tested. Once again, as a result of this agitation, expectations rose and reached new heights. How would the Government respond?

THE CRUCIAL MONTHS

Just when it looked as if the long battle was reaching its victorious climax, a new factor emerged to cast a shadow on the scene. The Germans had recently announced a programme of naval expansion. The demand went up for Britain to reply by spending millions more on the navy, even if it meant raiding the funds 'earmarked' for pensions. Battleships before pensions! It was rumoured that the Cabinet was split and that the First Lord of the Admiralty had threatened to resign unless the money for pensions was turned over to building more warships. After the experience, eight years earlier, of how the Boer War had torpedoed pension prospects, such rumours could not be taken lightly. Rev Stead was prompted by them to write to the journal *Review of Reviews* on the subject of 'the prospects and politics of pensions'. This important statement, which the journal's Editor described as a Manifesto, included the following:

1908 promises to be a great year. Unless incalculable accident or inconceivable stupidity intervene, the new year is bound to see the enactment of Old Age Pensions. The Government has pledged itself beyond all powers of withdrawal to legislate on the question in the approaching session. It has both the voting power and the financial resources equal to the task. And even if it had not the will, it is faced with forces which make inaction or postponement all but impossible. We may confidently count on 1908 becoming famous for the first Old Age Pensions Act passed within the United Kingdom.

Then he went on to deal with the rumours:

It is scarcely conceivable that so splendid an opportunity will be flung away . . . Ministers may be strengthened in their resolve to do justice to the aged by a glance at what would happen if they weakened or faltered or went back on their word. And there have been rumours that a sub-committee of the Cabinet, with Mr McKenna in the chair, has been considering the possibilities widely at variance from the definite pledges enumerated above. There are, moreover, vague impressions abroad that certain powerful financial interests, which work in darkness, are opposed to the readjustment of the national expenditure which would follow on a large measure of Old Age Pensions, and are exercising pressure of a kind that may not be seen in the open.

He then dealt with 'the whisper (that) has gone about' referring to proposals for means-testing and generally diluting the scheme backed by the public. Then he gave warning as to the consequences of delay or watering down the agreed principles. Pointing to recent by-election results he singled out Colne Valley as an example which *would be repeated in any number of industrial constituencies*, adding:

The working men have not forgotten that last year by remitting 3d off the income tax on earned incomes, and postponing pensions, Mr Asquith set the additional comfort of the comfortable classes before the admittedly urgent needs of the poor. No excuse of naval programme, or of any other kind, would prevent the conviction gaining ground that a Liberal Government cares only for the middle classes, and persistently sacrifices to them the interests of the working classes.

In conclusion he added that *any vacillation, or irresolution, or petty proposals would be politically damaging to the Liberal Party and give their Conservative opponents another opportunity of 'dishing the Whigs'* (a reference to when Disraeli won working class support for the Conservatives by bringing in a Reform Act after the Liberals had dithered and failed to do so). *As yet, however,* he said, *the cards are all in Liberal hands . . . But in any case the aged must have their pension.*

Advance copies of this Manifesto were sent to members of the Cabinet and to the leaders of the opposition. Acknowledgements were received, some formal, others expressing serious interest. The Viceroy of Ireland, Lord Aberdeen, wrote: *Most heartily do I hope that your words may have a stimulating and enlightening influence.*

The state opening of the next session of Parliament was on 29th January 1908. Those who had so long and valiantly striven for a measure of justice for a most needy section of the population now looked to the King's Speech. Would it bring another disappointment or would it fulfil their hopes? This was the moment of truth, and here is how Herbert Stead describes it: *Business took me on that day to the Strand terminus of the Hampstead Tube. There I saw the first evening newspaper announcing the King's Speech. To purchase a copy and glance through the lengthy report of the royal pronouncement was the work of a second. It was there!*

A BILL AT LAST!

It was in the King's Speech at last — the official guarantee of the enactment of old age pensions. It followed 11 paragraphs dealing with foreign and colonial affairs. It preceded the announcement of 11 separate Bills.

Unlike the Bills addressed to 'My Lords and Gentlemen' it was exclusively addressed to 'Gentlemen of the House of Commons'. This meant it was going to be a Money Bill which the Lords would not easily be able to sabotage. Its text read:

Estimates for the expenditure of the year will in due course be laid before you. In connection with the financial arrangements of the year, proposals will be brought forward for making better provision for old age, and legislation with that object will be submitted. On 22nd April 1908 the Prime Minister, Sir Henry Campbell-Bannerman, died. Although he is not now remembered in connection with the Old Age Pensions Act, it was largely due to his influence that the Government accepted the commitment to universal pensions. He was succeeded by Herbert Asquith, the former Chancellor.

It so happened that the Browning Settlement, which provided the National Pensions Committee with its headquarters, was inaugurated in 1895 with an address by the new Prime Minister. The annual meeting of the Settlement on 9th April sent him a message of congratulation in which there was a reminder of that occasion.

The Old Age Pensions Bill was now a priority in the Government's legislation programme but its terms still remained to be seen. Then, still to come, was the Parliamentary process with all its stages, during which changes for better or worse could be made, before there was an Act to go on the Statute Book.

The new Prime Minister, until so recently still the Chancellor, introduced the 'Old Age Pension Budget' with a speech which surveyed the whole financial scene, including the Government's intentions with regard to pensions. The speech reflected a buoyant financial situation.

There had been an unprecedented reduction of £18 million in the national debt. Despite the 3d off income tax, revenue had soared. The actual surplus in hand was greatly in excess of the amount estimated. This was a very healthy basis on which to turn to the question of pensions.

He began with a sympathetic reference to *the figure of old age, still unprovided for except by casual and unorganised effort, or, by what is worse, invidious dependence on Poor Law relief.* Then followed a Westminster-eye view of the pensions agitation, outlining some of the early schemes, the 1895 Royal Commission (which had been totally negative), Lord Rothschild's Committee, the Select Committee of 1899, a Departmental Committee of 1900, and another Select Committee in 1903. All this, he said, produced much valuable material, but . . . *up to this moment nothing has been done; nothing at all.* A glaring omission in his survey was the entire effort outside Parliament without which there would have been little or no Parliamentary interest in the issue. He made no mention of Charles Booth's pioneering work which stimulated such massive working class support and gave rise to the National Committee of Organised Labour. Nor did he refer to that Committee's eight years of vigorous and effective campaigning. This blind spot in Mr Asquith's speech led Rev Stead to comment: *There is something very delightful about the way Parliament affects not to know what is going on outside Parliament.*

Mr Asquith proceeded cautiously to declare that he had only promised to make a beginning, and to advance tentatively and by stages. Only then did he unveil the Government's intentions. Pensions were to be placed, he said *once and for all outside both the machinery and associations of our Poor Law system.* Then he ruled out so-called contributory systems. After this promising start he went on to pour cold water on *the universal scheme associated with the name of Mr Charles Booth* [which] *is also out of the range of practical politics.* This attack on the principles of Mr Booth's scheme, which was embodied in the policy of the National Committee, contrasted with the tributes paid to Mr Booth by other Ministers and Members. It was an attack which sought to cover his retreat from the principle of universality which he had previously accepted. He went on to say that the full cost of the scheme would be borne by the State, and that eligibility for a pension would depend on residence in the UK and not on tests of character.

• The amount of pensions was to be 5/- weekly, subject to an income limit.

• Single people with a weekly income of over 10/- (50p) would be ruled out; married couples whose joint income exceeded 15/- (75p) would also be ruled out.

- The starting age for entitlement was to be 70.
- Conviction for serious crime within the previous five years would also disqualify.
- Payment would be through the Post Office: the first pensions would be paid on New Year's Day 1909.

There was some doubt as to how many people would actually qualify for this provision but the maximum actual annual cost was expected to be less than £6 million. As the scheme would only become operative the following January, the estimated cost in the current financial year was only £1,200,000. When that amount is compared with the *at least £2,500,000 earmarked for pensions* in the same financial year as previously announced, the grudging attitude of the Government was all too obvious. Rubbing salt into the wound, Mr Asquith then announced that there was still a surplus of £3,700,000 nearly all of which went on a reduction of the sugar duty by one farthing in the pound.

There was an immediate reaction from the Parliamentary Labour Party to Mr Asquith's failure to honour the principle of universality. On the evening of the Budget speech, Arthur Henderson read out in the House the authorised report of Mr Campbell-Bannerman and Mr Asquith's speeches on 20th November 1906, when the former stated: *any scheme must be universal in its application* — a view which the latter *entirely endorsed*.

The verdict of the National Committee was expressed in a circular four days after the budget. It welcomed all the positive aspects of the Government's proposals as being in line with what they had fought for, but refered to its failure on the principle of universality as in contradiction to its own commitment. It went on to press for immediate action to raise the income limit (from £26 a year), and to lower the starting age from 70 to 65. Attention was also drawn to the breach of faith by the Government which, having promised at least £2½ million, was now proposing to spend less than half that sum.

ENTER LLOYD GEORGE

It was only at this point that Lloyd George, as the new Chancellor of
the Exchequer in succession to Mr Asquith, became involved with the
Government's Old Age Pensions Bill. The First Reading was on 28th
May and on 2nd June the Bill's text was published. The new Chancellor now became responsible for the Bill's passage through Parliament.

A PRESENTATION MILLSTONE

Mr Asquith 'It is my pleasant duty, my dear Lloyd George, to hand
on to you this trinket presented to me by a grateful country. I need
hardly ask you to be worthy of it.'

[May 27, 1908]

81

The first public reaction to the news that at last provision was to be made for old people was one of great satisfaction. The mood changed when the terms of the Bill became known. Serious dissatisfaction was expressed about the wide range of disqualifying clauses it contained, and also about some of the administrative provisions. Clause 3 excluded from eligibility for pension people *in receipt of any such parochial or other relief as disqualifies for registration as a Parliamentary elector.* The phrase *or other relief* could be very widely applied, as was pointed out by George Barnes in the Second Reading debate. Lloyd George promptly agreed to remove the offending phrase. Another paragraph disqualified anybody who had been *brought into a position to apply for a pension through his own wilful act or misbehaviour.* This, too, was in contradiction to previous Government policy. It was aggravated by another provision which allowed members of the Charity Organisation Society to be co-opted to local Pension Committees. They would seek to interpret the disqualification clause in the harshest possible manner. The Government yielded to pressure on the character-test clause but retained the co-option provision. Fortunately, as a result of changes in the disqualification rules little scope remained for those co-opted.

The Second Reading debate was on 15th and 16th June. It was opened by Lloyd George whose speech reflected his newness to his brief, though also his capacity to master it. He showed some flexibility when changes in the Bill were proposed. For example, he undertook to consider replacing the fixed income limit by a sliding scale. True to their previous attitude, the Tory opposition objected to the proposed spending of taxpayers' money on pensions. Their leader, Lord Robert Cecil, said it was a case of throwing away to the aged the funds that might be needed in a life and death struggle for national existence.

The MPs associated with the National Committee went out of their way to pay tribute to the work of Charles Booth on behalf of the aged, work which, at least in part, was bearing fruit in the House.

This helped to make good Mr Asquith's failure to give credit to Booth and also to spotlight the deficiencies in the Bill. When the vote was taken on an opposition amendment it mustered only 29 votes with a massive 417 against it, including 43 Conservatives. Then the Second Reading was carried without a division.

Before the Bill could become law there was still the Committee Stage, the Report Stage and the Third Reading. The day after the Second Reading the Chancellor made clear that he meant business. He brought in a resolution to limit the Committee Stage to five days, the Report Stage and Third Stage to one day each. 178 amendments had already been tabled and the final number could be double that. To adhere to his timetable he proposed the guillotine procedure which would cut short the debate. He argued that in principle the House was agreed: there were only five points of serious controversy, namely:

1) The age limit;

2) The sliding scale question;

3) Possible reduction of pensions for old couples living together;

4) The industry test;

5) The pauper disqualification.

For 1), 2) and 3) he would allow 1½ days; for 4) and 5) another 1½ days; plus an extra day for the machinery of administration. These proposals were accepted by 306 votes to 202.

The Committee Stage began on 23rd June. An amendment in favour of a sliding scale was carried. This scale meant that only those with an income of less than 8/- weekly would get the full pension of 5/- weekly; between 8/- and 9/- weekly income the pension was reduced by 1/- to 4/- weekly; then likewise in 1/- stages until there was no pension for anyone whose income exceeded 12/- weekly. Although it was estimated that this scale would add £110,000 to the total cost of the scheme, the National Committee opposed it as a backward step.

The terms of the Bill provided that couples would receive only 3/9 each instead of 5/-. This led to a highly charged debate, with 22 amendments demanding the deletion of this clause tabled by Members in all parts of the House. Speakers in support of these amendments objected to the idea that Darby and Joan should be penalised because on reaching pension age they were still living together. The feeling in the House crossed party boundaries. The Conservative MP, F E Smith, saw an opportunity to embarrass the Government. *Note the piety of our Government,* he said. *They give you 7/6 a week for living with your own wife and 10/- for living with somebody else's.* It was generally expected that the Government would retreat on this issue but its spokesman, Mr McKenna, stood firm. He just repeated the old argument that a couple required less than two separate persons, and that anyway, the Government could not afford any more money. This provoked such consternation in the House that the Government was compelled to give way. Lloyd George rose to announce the surrender — on condition that the House made no further financial demands in respect of the Bill.

Because of the guillotine procedure which curtailed debate, there was no time to discuss amendments which would have reduced the qualifying age to 65. So 70 it remained. The tight-fistedness of the Government was further revealed when the issue of those in receipt of Poor Law relief was discussed. There was strong pressure for the Bill not to disqualify them from receiving pensions. Again the Chancellor pleaded lack of funds but finally conceded that the disqualification would cease in December 1910.

After the Committee Stage was completed the Bill was considered on Report on 7th July, followed by the Third Reading on 9th July. There was only one day for this during which the whole range of attitudes to the proposed legislation was voiced. Making its main target the non-contributory character of the scheme, an opposition amendment involving its rejection was moved. Others complained about the abandonment of universality, and the remaining grounds for disqualification. These included: *If, before he becomes entitled*

*to a pension, he has habitually failed to work according to his
ability, opportunity and need, for the maintenance or benefit of
himself and those legally dependent on him.* A powerful speech
was made by Charles Masterman, a Liberal MP. He exposed various weaknesses in the Bill and later Lloyd George conceded his
case but defended the Government's position, saying: *By excluding
all alternatives, we are driven to establish certain limitations,*

THE PHILANTHROPIC HIGHWAYMAN

Mr Lloyd George 'I'll make 'em pity the aged poor!'

[August 5,1908]

which we acknowledge are illogical, against which strong batter-
ies of reason can be advanced, and on the border lines of which
anomalies are left; but we only declare, laying all our cards upon
the table, and acknowledging these anomalies and limitations, that
it is better that we should go forward with the money at our
disposal than that we should do nothing at all.

The Labour MPs spoke out strongly, defending the Bill against Tory opposition but highlighting its weaknesses. They asked the House to accept the Bill as an instalment with which they were not going to rest content. The closure was applied at 10.30 pm and the final division was taken. It soon became clear that the amendment had attracted only derisory support, and the voting figures were: FOR the amendment 10; AGAINST 315. Included in the majority vote were 12 Conservatives, the remainder abstaining. Of the 10 who voted for the amendment, five represented university constituencies (since abolished), one represented the City of London, and one was the son of the former Conservative Chancellor, Michael Hicks-Beach (since elevated to the peerage). After this fiasco for the amendment the Third Reading was put and carried.

LAST DITCH OPPOSITION BY THE LORDS

There was still another hurdle to face before the Bill could receive the Royal Assent and become the law of the land. It was now the turn of the House of Lords to debate the Bill, though they could not tamper with its overall financial provisions. The Lords' First Reading was on 10th July, followed by the Second Reading on

20th July. It soon became clear that it was not going to be plain sailing. After Lord Wolverhampton moved the Second Reading for the Government, the Earl of Wemyss moved an amendment, *That pending the report of the Royal Commission now enquiring into the principles of the existing Poor Law, it would be unwise to enter upon the consideration of a Bill establishing the far-reaching principle of state old age pensions.* Of special interest was the speech of the Archbishop of Canterbury. *The time for action,* he said, *had arrived; the results would conduce in the highest degree to the common good of the English people.* He paid eloquent tribute to the work of Charles Booth — *There is one whose name has, I think, had too scanty justice done to it in the course of debates on this Bill — I refer to Mr Charles Booth . . . Some fifteen years have passed since he published his great work . . . upon* **The Condition of the Aged Poor.** *The 500 pages or so of that book, containing so many facts and figures, set forth so impartially, in a manner so intelligible and of course so readable that no book of the same dimensions written upon any subject is comparable to it.*

Looked at from today the provisions of the Bill were modest in the extreme, and less than adequate in a whole number of respects. Yet, in the Lords debate, Lord Roseberry could say of that same Bill: *Speaking from the bottom of my heart I believe this is the most important Bill, by a long way, that has ever been submitted to the House of Lords during the forty years that I have sat in it. I view its consequences as so great, so mystic, so incalculable, so largely affecting the whole scope and fabric of our Empire itself, that I rank it as a measure far more vitally important than even the great Reform Bills which have come before this House.* After that tribute he went on, while not asking for its rejection, to express reservations about the Bill! The vote on the Second Reading of the Bill carried by 123 votes to 16. This did not mean it was acceptable to the Lords. Indeed, had it not been a Money Bill it would have been severely manhandled. The Peers' deep hostility surfaced when they reached the Committee Stage on 28th July.

Lord Cromer (former Consul General of Egypt which, effectively, he had ruled as a British possession) had given notice to amend Clause 1 of the Bill by limiting its operation to 31st December 1915. The Lord Chancellor, for the Government, gave warning that this, and many other amendments, would be regarded as an infringement of the privileges of the Commons. He urged the Peers to pass the amendment and leave with the Commons the responsibility for rejection. This they did by a vote of 77 to 45. After some other hostile amendments were carried the mutilated Bill completed the Committee Stage in the Lords. On the following two days it went through the Report Stage and, as amended, passed its Third Reading. Then it went back to the Commons.

Here Lord Cromer, a member of the Barings, the powerful banking family, got his come-uppance from Will Crooks, the former workhouse inmate now a Labour MP. Will Crooks solemnly gave notice that on an early day he proposed to move, *That having regard to the fact that this House recently voted £50,000 to Lord Cromer, it is of opinion that he does not stand in need of a Government pension of £900 per annum, and that it should cease on and after 1st January 1915.* The House exploded with mirth, which echoed throughout the press and the nation at large. The retort of Will Crooks also made a serious point about the pensions of peers and the poor, as well as asserting the powers of the House of Commons to deal with both.

Will Crooks' intervention was the prelude to the proceedings in the Commons which met on 31st July to consider the Bill as amended by the Lords. The Speaker quickly ruled that the amendments of Lord Cromer and some others were in breach of Commons privilege. Some Lords amendments were accepted but these were of a technical nature not affecting any matter of substance. The Commons had dealt with the Lords in a confident, resolute, even defiant manner. It then sent its message, explaining the fate of their amendments, to the Lords.

The end of the last act of the great drama of the long battle for the Old Age Pension Act was now at hand. All the Lords could do was to perform a face-saving exercise. Lord Cromer, apparently chastened by the publicity resulting from Will Crooks' initiative, disavowed any hostility to the Bill, and moved that the Lords do not insist on his amendment. It was left to Lord Landsdowne, as a final gesture, to move that while not insisting on its amendments, the Lords did not accept the Commons' reasons for rejecting them or as a precedent for the future. His motion was carried by the meagre vote of 37 to 23. So, ungracious to the bitter end the House of Lords was compelled to submit to the Commons — which itself had been forced, without an excess of grace, to yield at last to the popular will.

THE LESSONS — FOR THEN AND FOR TODAY

Next day, on 1st August 1908, the House reassembled at noon and the Royal Assent was given to the Old Age Pensions Act. The historic deed was done. Implementation of the Act would begin on New Year's Day 1909.

Looking back on the ten years of hard labour which had proved to be the price of achieving the Act, Rev Francis Herbert Stead, Warden of the Browning Settlement and Hon Secretary of the National Committee of Organised Labour from the beginning until the end, drew these conclusions[1]:

1) But for the independent agitation described above, neither the Conservative nor the Liberal Party would have enacted Old Age Pensions.

2) That a reform of such magnitude should have arrived at the verge of legislative settlement without the official aid of either party is in itself a marvel needing to be explained. The story told here provides that explanation.

3) The vision inspired initially by the principles presented by Charles Booth evoked a response which united a wide cross-section of the population despite their differences on other issues. That unity was made effective by the National Committee of Organised Labour. (With characteristic modesty he does not refer to his own role, but singles out the Organising Secretary, Frederick Rogers, as the personification of the Committee's purpose). The principal forces mobilised by the National Committee were, firstly, those of organised Labour, and next those of organised religion.

4) Success in organising grass-roots support brought the issue of pensions *to the threshold of Parliament.* To make it a live issue in the House it was necessary to have the backing of MPs and a party inside Parliament. In the earlier phase of the campaign this was lacking, except for some of the Labour Members of the Liberal

Party. The foundation of the Labour Representation Committee (of which Frederick Rogers was the first Chairman) paved the way for the formation of the Parliamentary Labour Party which gave priority to the fight for *Pensions for all in old age*. With the arrival of MPs like Will Crooks, and later George Barnes, Chairman of the National Committee and the Labour Party's 'Shadow' Minister for Pensions, the pressure on Parliament from outside was united with Parliamentary pressure and leadership from within.

5) Despite the vital contribution of the Labour Party, pensions were more than a party issue. The movement led by the National Committee comprised 'good people of all parties, or none' both outside and inside Parliament. The leadership of the National Committee never became superfluous. (In fact, after the passing of the Act the Committee continued in existence and agitated for the full reform of which the Act was seen as only the first instalment).

6) Despite its momentous character, the ten year agitation was conducted on a shoestring budget. The accounts of the National Committee of Organised Labour show an average yearly expenditure of no more than £400 (including the full-time organiser's wages).

7) The cause of the aged poor brought out the best in all those who joined the fight for pensions and gave an added ethical dimension to the movement.

8) This ethical character was reflected in the whole record of decisions taken with virtual unanimity by people prepared to shelve doubts and differences in order to put basic principles first.

9) From first to last the movement stood by its principles and policy. Instalments were accepted; co-operation, even if incomplete, welcomed; but never at the price of departing from the programme of the National Committee.

10) The actual arrival of pensions had a dual reaction. On the one hand, despite the long agitation (perhaps partly because of it), the outcome still came as a surprise to many in public life. On the other hand, pensions quickly became assimilated to the national life as a matter of course.

11) Pensions introduced an elemental change into the life of the nation, a change widely acknowledged to be revolutionary. It was followed, in 1909, by further radical social legislation embodied in the 'People's Budget' of Lloyd George. The effect on people's hopes and expectations was dramatic. In the words of Rev Stead: *Not with the bursting of bombs, not with the click of the guillotine, but with the quiet handing over in innumerable post offices of a weekly couple of half crowns has the English revolution of the twentieth century begun.*

12) As a profoundly religious man, Rev Stead saw in the successful outcome of the struggle some help from outside, divine intervention in response to prayer.

Five months after the passing of the Act, its first beneficiaries began to draw their pensions. It was fitting that in Walworth, the cradle of the agitation, the first Sunday in 1909 was designated Pensions Thanksgiving Sunday. Leaflets and posters invited the aged pensioners of Walworth to join in a Service of Thanks at Browning Hall, *the headquarters of the pension movement.*

Nationally, when the scheme came into force, over half a million of the aged collected pensions. In the Borough of Southwark, which includes Walworth, no less than 1,700 had drawn their first couple of half crowns. Sunday proved to be a miserable day — wet, foggy and muddy. Yet despite age and feebleness a hundred pensioners braved the terrors of foggy streets, muddy roads and wet clothes. They were welcomed at the Settlement with an orchestra, tea and cake. They formed a pathetic but joyous spectacle, the battered veterans of poverty who had won the long fight against the dread of pauperism. With deep emotion they said to Rev Stead, *You promised us a pension, and they said we never should get it. But now we've got it. You spoke true. God bless you!*

After the singing and prayer there was a meeting addressed by Frederick Rogers. In greeting what had been achieved, he called for an extension of the provisions — the abolition of the pauper disqualification and the sliding scale, and the lowering of the age limit to 65.

The Walworth celebration was symptomatic of the national reaction. As the Chancellor who got the lion's share of press publicity, it was Lloyd George who got most of the credit for the Old Age Pensions Act. As Flora Thompson records in her book, Lark Rise, many pensioners when collecting their 5/- from the post office said: *God bless Lord George!* They could not believe that such a miracle could be the work of a mere 'Mister'. In fact to many pensioners their weekly income became known as their 'Lloyd George' (or as one the characters in Dorothy Sayers' *Nine Tailors* calls it, 'Lord George'.)

As the years have rolled by since 1908, the history books have continued to remember Lloyd George (who did indeed become an Earl in the fullness of time), while those more truly deserving of remembrance have faded into oblivion. The 90th anniversary of the passing of the Act affords today's well-organised and influential pensioner movement an opportunity to make amends and set the record straight. A wide ranging commemoration would be an opportunity to recall the long battle for the Act and to pay tribute to the forgotten men and women whose vision, fighting ability and sheer determination, finally won the day. Those same qualities are still needed if what has been won in the past is not to be lost in the future. In recent years there has been serious erosion of hard-won gains. The writing is on the wall unless the challenge is met.

There are many lessons to be learnt from this story. One of them is that war and preparation for war are the enemy of social progress. Had it not been for the Boer War pensions would have been won years sooner. If the Act had been delayed beyond 1908 the clamour for more battleships and the arms race which culminated, in 1914, in the First World War would have created a climate increasingly hostile to social reform. When, then, would pensions have come? That is why this story of the battle for pensions, 1898-1908, is also a story for today.

(1) *How Old Age Pensions Began To Be* by Francis Herbert Stead, 1910 Methuen

ORGANISED LABOUR AND THE PENSION FIGHT

Organised Labour played a leading role in the 10 year campaign to secure the Old Age Pension Act in 1908. 80 years later, on 22 September 1988, at the headquarters of the London Labour Party, on the site of Browning Hall, the pension campaign headquarters, the Rt Hon Neil Kinnock MP, Leader of the Labour Party, unveiled a plaque in honour of the pioneers who led the fight for the pension. This ceremony was followed by a packed Pensioner Rally at the North Peckham Civic Centre addressed by Neil Kinnock, Jack Jones and Dave Goodman. Here are some extracts from the speech of Neil Kinnock:

(The introduction of the pension) was a great and progressive change. And, of course, it was strongly opposed by powerful vested interests. They said it would discourage thrift and encourage idleness; that it was too expensive; that it would destroy private provision . . . Those arguments should be historic relics . . . Tragically they aren't. We hear them today. They come from the Thatcher throwbacks.

Only one thing can really halt the robbing of the older generation and that is the election of Governments pledged to establish and sustain a decent, liveable level of basic pensions . . . a Government committed to re-establishing the link with earnings and restoring and improving the State Earnings Related Pension for men and for women . . . (as) part of a strategy to ensure that retirement is a time of dignity, security, activity, choice and real freedom for all people and of dependence for none. And such a strategy will only come from a Labour Government. That is the pledge that we make.

That pledge was reaffirmed by John Smith, Leader of the Labour Party, in a speech to thousands of pensioners at a Westminster Central Hall Rally. He received a standing ovation.

Plaque unveiled by Jack Jones on October 12, 1988, at the birthplace of Francis Herbert Stead at a North Tyneside civic ceremony to mark the 80th anniversary of the introduction to Britain of the State Old Age Pension

Photo by Stan Gamester

 Other books from
Third Age Press
the independent publishing company
inspired by older people

*A little of what you fancy does you good: your health
in later life*   Dr H B Gibson   **£8.50**
'Wise guidance to make the most of your later years'
(Dr Stanway, Woman's Weekly)

On the tip of your tongue: your memory in later life
~ our best seller!   Dr H B Gibson   **£7.00**

Changes and challenges in later life: learning from experience
Yvonne Craig (ed). Foreword by Claire Rayner ~ how to
transform 'surviving into thriving'.   **£10.00**

Consider the alternatives: healthy strategies for later life ~
clear, unbiased information on complementary medicine &
alternative therapies. Caroline Nash with Tony Carter   **£10.00**

Voyage of Rediscovery: a guide to writing your life story
Eric Midwinter   **£4.00**

The Rhubarb People ~ Eric Midwinter's funny & poignant
memoir of 1930s Manchester   **£4.00 (or £5.00 on cassette)**

Lifescapes: the landscape of a lifetime   Enid Irving
Create a collage that illustrates a life ~ for groups or individuals
£4.00

All prices include p & p   Cheques to   Third Age Press
6 Parkside Gardens,   London SW19 5EY